The letters **a**, **e**, **i**, **o**, and **u** are vowels.

a, e, i, o, u

Vowels can be **short vowels** or **long vowels**.
Long vowels sound like themselves when said aloud.
Circle the **long vowels** in these words:

cake key pie boat glue

Short vowels make a different sound.
Circle the **short vowels** in these words:

cat sled pig fox sun

Consonants are all of the letters of the alphabet that are not vowels.

b, c, d, f, g, h, j, k, l, m, n, p, q, r, s, t, v, w, x, y, z

Cross out the **consonants** in these words:

dog fish zebra

Tammy Turtle is looking for **t** words.
Write the **t** words for the pictures.

ten tie toys tub tiger tent

1.

2.

3.

4.

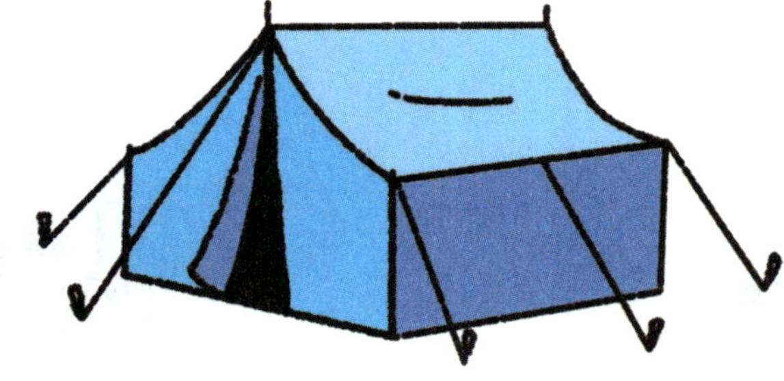

5.

6.

Circle the **t** words in the word search.

tub toys tail top turtle
tomato tiger turkey

T	U	R	K	E	Y	A	H	X	A	W
F	W	X	J	L	A	L	G	A	T	C
T	X	T	O	Y	S	K	U	C	I	A
O	Y	A	C	D	J	Z	J	A	G	X
M	N	L	A	T	Y	W	T	A	E	M
A	A	T	S	O	K	X	V	K	R	F
T	H	A	G	P	H	P	W	A	J	P
O	K	I	D	A	O	T	U	B	G	L
V	A	L	C	I	H	X	D	M	K	N
U	Y	X	K	T	U	R	T	L	E	J

Help Monkey Meg get to the moon.
Write the **m** words by the pictures.

map mice moon
mouse monkey milk

Read the clues.
Write the **m** answers in the puzzle.

moon man map
money mouse mop

Across

1. I am smaller than a rat.
2. You see me at night.
3. I clean floors.

Down

1. Your father is one.
2. I help you find places.
3. You need me to buy things.

1.

2.

3.

CONSONANT: b

Busy Bee is looking for **b** words.
Write the **b** words for the pictures.

bell **bug** **bed** **bird** **ball** **book**

1. ______________________

2. ______________________

3. ______________________

4. ______________________

5. ______________________

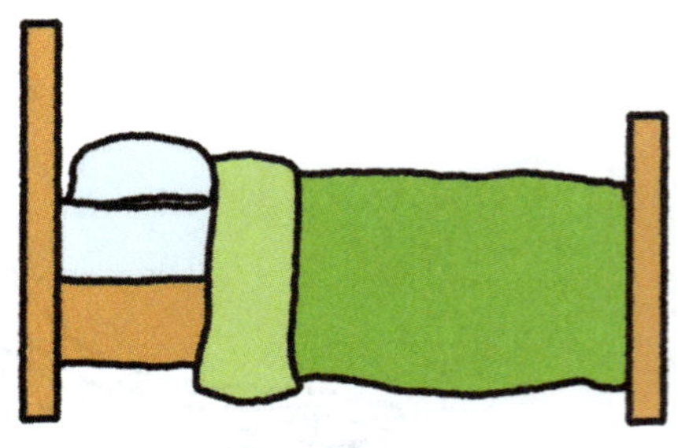

6. ______________________

CONSONANT: b

Circle the **b** words in the word search.

bug boy bus bear boat banana balloon baby

B	U	B	K	B	O	Y	H	X	B	W
O	M	U	J	L	A	L	G	A	A	C
A	X	G	O	Y	B	U	S	C	N	A
T	Y	A	C	D	J	I	J	C	A	X
M	N	L	X	B	A	B	Y	A	N	M
B	E	A	R	O	A	U	V	K	A	F
T	B	A	L	L	O	O	N	A	J	P
E	K	L	O	A	O	T	W	B	G	L

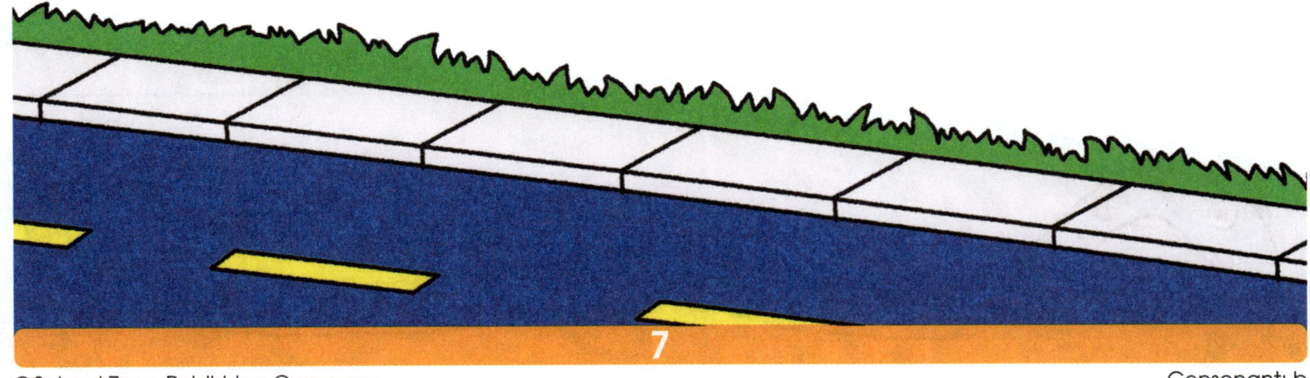

CONSONANT: s

Sammy Snake is looking for solutions.
Write the **s** answers to the riddles.

sun soap seal snake seven sand

1. This helps you keep clean.
2. You play on me at the beach.
3. I am a number.
4. I have flippers and live in the water.
5. I keep the earth warm.
6. I move without legs.

Help the ship get to the shore.
Write the **s** words by the pictures.
Be careful! One word does not belong.

ship shore sandals
sun soap socks duck

Polly Parrot is leading the **p** parade.
Write the **p** words for the pictures.

pie pear pig pony puppy penny

1. ______________________

2. ______________________

3. ______________________

4. ______________________

5. ______________________

6. ______________________

Circle the **p** words in the word search.

paint park party pail
panda pizza puzzle peanut pony

Help Leon Lion get to his ladder.
Write the **l** words by the pictures.
Be careful! One word does not belong.

watermelon		lion
lock	ladder	lamp
lemon	letter	lamb

Write the **l** words by the pictures.

lion leaf lock lamb letter lemon

1. ______________________

2. ______________________

3. ______________________

4. ______________________

5. ______________________

6. ______________________

Meet Nothing. He eats **n** words.
Then there will be nothing!

next nothing
name night never

Help! The words got all mixed up.
Unscramble the **n** words.

1. emna

2. enerv

3. xtne

4. ghtni

5. nhnotgi

Read the clues.
Write the **n** answers in the puzzle.

Across

1. What you are called is your_____ .
2. It holds wood together.
3. Birds make_____ .
4. You smell with your_____ .

Down

1. It is a coin worth five pennies.
2. It is the number before ten.
3. It tells how many.
4. It is the opposite of yes.

1.

2.

3.

4.

no
nail
nests
nine
nose
name
nickel
number

REVIEWING THE LETTERS t, m, b, s, p, l & n

Can you help Billy find his way out of the cave?
Write the words by the pictures.

ten bell pie tub map sun pig
nail leaf moon sand ball lock nine

REVIEWING THE LETTERS t, m, b, s, p, l & n

Circle the correct words to finish the sentences.

1. Did you get stung by a _____?

   bee **be** **bea**

2. I hope we get _____ in time for the party.

   their **they're** **there**

3. Did you _____ the letter?

   male **mayl** **mail**

4. My foot became _____ from wearing shoes that were too small.

   sore **soar** **soer**

5. Bring your shovel and _____ to the beach.

   pail **payl** **pale**

6. I'm tired and need to _____ down.

   lye **ley** **lie**

7. Make sure you tie a _____ in your bow.

   not **knot** **note**

REVIEWING THE LETTERS t, m, b, s, p, l & n

Help! The words got all mixed up.
Write the words for the pictures.

bed
tent
seal
lemon
moon
nickel
puppy

1. 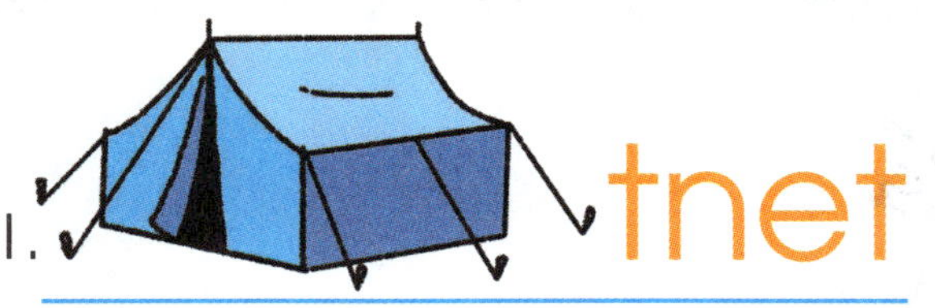 tnet

2.  omon

3. 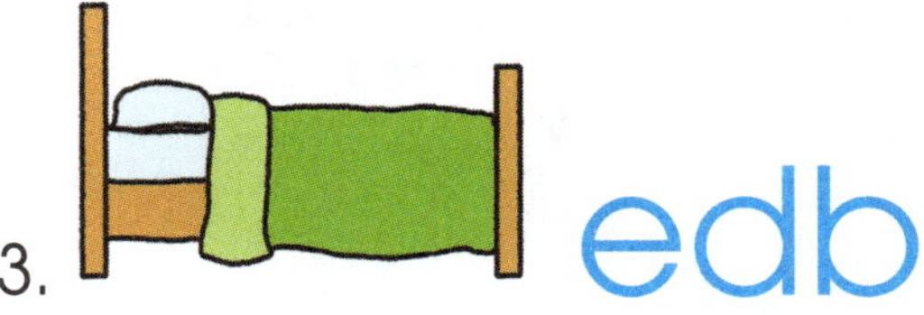 edb

4.  lsae

5.  emlon

6.  puypp

7. 

ncklei

CONSONANT: d

Write the **d** words for the pictures.

doll dog deer dime doctor dollar

1. ____________________

2. ____________________

3. ____________________

4. ____________________

5. ____________________

6. ____________________

Help! The words got all mixed up.
Write the **d** words for the pictures.

dew	dad
duck	desk
den	desert

1. ckud

2. sdek

3. nde

4. dtrese

5. wde

6. dda

CONSONANT: f

Write the **f** words for the pictures.

fox fish food fire farm feet

1.

2.

3.

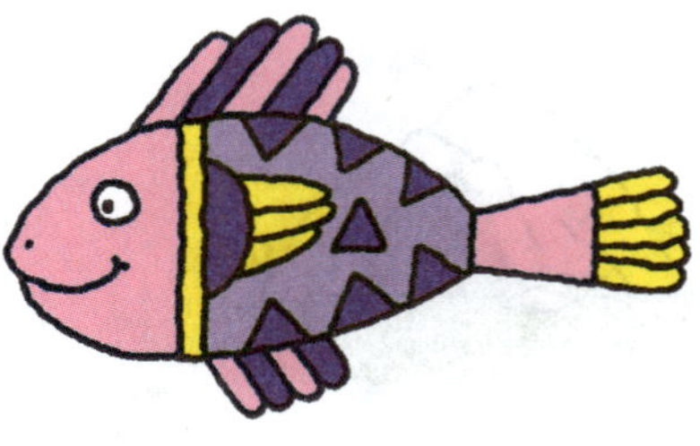

4.

5.

6.

CONSONANT: f

Help the firefighter get to the fire.
Write the **f** words by the pictures.
Be careful! One word does not belong.

fox fire firefighter food fish fan rabbit

Help Happy Horse get to the hay.
Write the **h** words by the pictures.

hay hill hat hen horse hand

Read the clues.
Write the **h** answers in the puzzle.

Across

1. I live in a white _____ .
2. Her _____ is in pigtails.
3. My dad wears a _____ .

Down

1. A _____ is bigger than a pony.
2. The valentine is shaped like a _____ .
3. I was _____ to see my old friend.

hair house heart horse hat happy

CONSONANT: r

Write the **r** words for the pictures.

rake red ring rose robin rabbit

1. ______

2. ______

3. ______

4. ______

5. ______

6. ______

R is for riddle.
Write the **r** answers to the riddles.

rain race red road rope

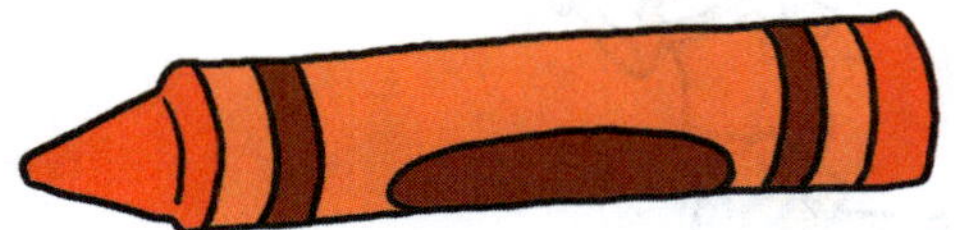

1. It is a color.

2. It is wet.

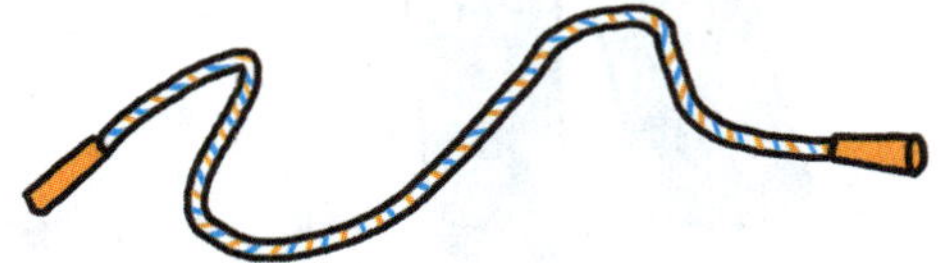

3. You can jump with it.

4. You can drive a car on it.

5. You can run in it.

Help! The words got all mixed up.
Write the **j** words for the pictures.

job jogger jail jeans jacket juggler

1. alij

2. rgogje

3. bjo

4. easnj

5. cketaj

6. uglrejg

Circle the **j** words in the word search.

joke just jet jug jacks jelly jar jump

Draw lines from the pictures to the words.
Then write the **k** words.

1. 

kitten ____________________

2. 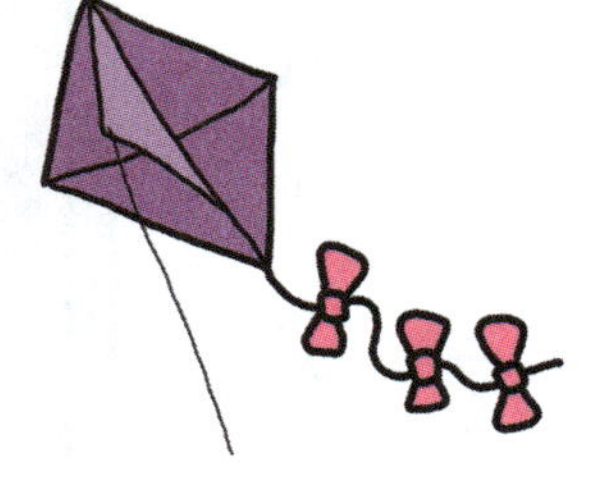

kite ____________________

3. 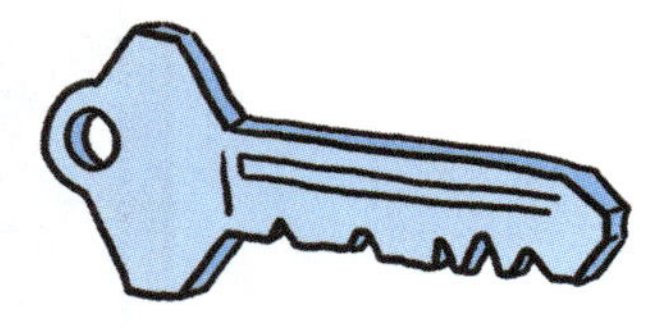

king ____________________

4. 

kiss ____________________

5. 

key ____________________

CONSONANT: k

Draw lines from the letters on the left to the letters on the right to complete the **k** words.

1.	kit	ck
2.	kn	te
3.	ki	ten
4.	ko	it
5.	ki	ala
6.	kn	ot
7.	kni	ght

Help Wally Worm wiggle to the watermelon.
Write the **w** words by the pictures.

web worm wolf watch
woman wagon watermelon

Help finish the words.
Circle the letters that make complete **w** words.

1.	we	tch	ar	are
2.	wa	lk	er	ess
3.	wh	tch	el	eat
4.	wi	ell	de	ed
5.	wo	od	d	uck
6.	wr	nd	els	ite
7.	wo	ld	man	nen

REVIEWING THE LETTERS d, f, h, r, j, k & w

Can you help the diver get to the treasure chest?
Write the words by the pictures.

doll dog fish hen hat fox jet
web kitten wagon rake ring jar kite

REVIEWING THE LETTERS d, f, h, r, j, k & w

Help! The words got all mixed up.
Write the words for the pictures.

key
fire
wolf
dime
robin
jacks
horse

1. 

imed

2.  rife

3.  heors

4.  obrni

5.  kcsaj

6. 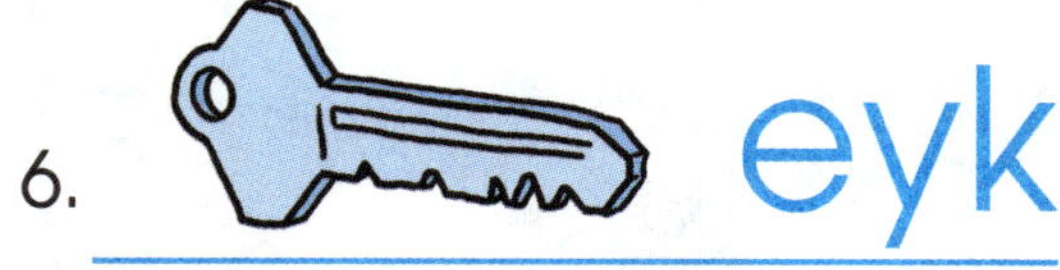 eyk

7.  wflo

Circle the correct words to finish the sentences.

1. How many_____are there in October?

   days   daze   dase

2. Can you go to the_____with me?

   fayr   fair   fare

3. The rabbits _____ into the hutch.

   hoped   hopped   houpt

4. The book was too hard to_____.

   reed   reid   read

5. Who_____the winning goal?

   kicked   kiked   kicted

6. Are you wearing new_____?

   genes   jeans   jeens

7. He was too_____to lift the chair.

   weak   week   weik

Which end with **y**?
Circle the **y** words and pictures.

1. girl big funny

2.

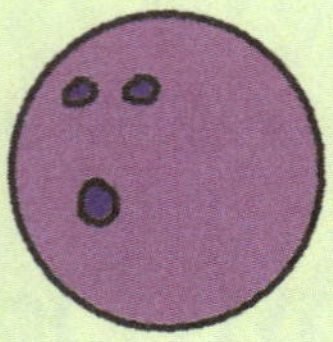

3. tiger why never

4.

5. fun game play

6.

7. sad happy like

8.

Circle the **y** words in the word search.

Help! The words got all mixed up.
Write the **v** words for the pictures.

violin vine van vest vacuum violet

1.  iolniv

2.  nevi

3.  anv

4.  estv

5.  vmucua

6.  itelov

CONSONANT: v

Valerie Vole is looking for **v** words.
Circle the **v** words in the word search.

vase violin valentine vegetable vest van

Write the **z** words for the pictures.

zipper **zoo** **zebra** **zero**

1.

2.

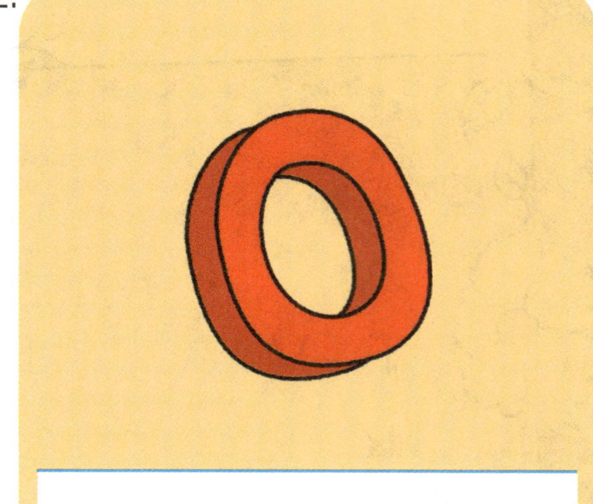

3.

4.

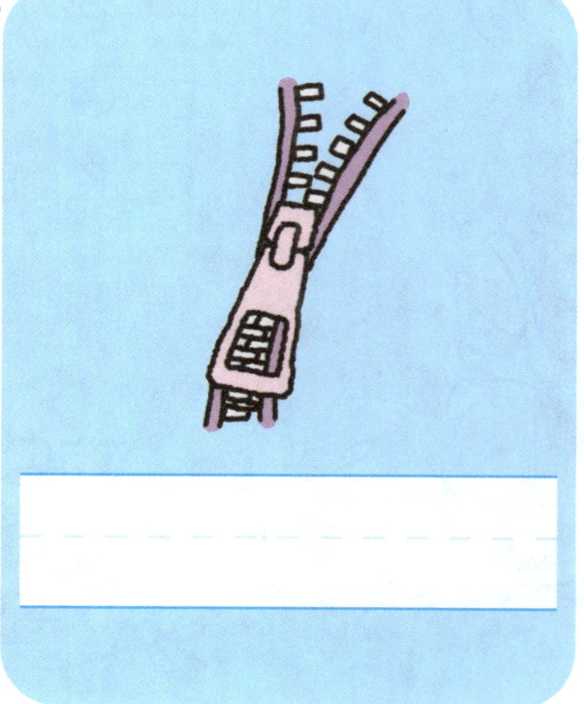

Draw lines from the pictures to the words.
Then write the **z** words.

1. 

zoo

2. 

zero

3. 

zebra

4. 

zipper

5. 

zucchini

Write the **q** words to finish the sentences.

quilt quail queen quarter

1. My sister looks like a ____________ .

2. The toy cost a ____________ .

3. The ____________ keeps me warm.

4. A ____________ is a wild bird.

5. Draw pictures of as many things that begin with **q** as you can.

Draw lines from the pictures to the words.
Then write the **q** words.

1. 

quarter ____________________

2. 

queen ____________________

3. 

quill ____________________

4. 

quilt ____________________

5. 

quail ____________________

Write the **c** words for the pictures.

circus center city circles

1.

2.

3.

4.

Circle the **c** words in the word search.

cake corn cat cow coat cup camel

When **g** is used with **e**, **i**, or **y**, it has a soft sound.
It sounds like the **g** in giraffe.

Connect the dots and color the picture to finish General Giant Giraffe.
Then trace and write the **g** words.

1. general

2. giant

3. giraffe

Read the clues.
Write the **g** answers in the puzzle.

goat game girl
gold goose gate

Across

1. Dad went to the baseball _____ with Danny.
2. The _____ to the dog pen is locked.
3. Mom lost her _____ watch.

Down

1. Does a _____ have horns?
2. Meg's mother had a baby _____ .
3. A _____ is a bird.

CONSONANT: x

Sometimes **x** is at the end of a word.
Write the **x** words for the pictures.

box fox six ax

1.

2.

3.

4.

REVIEW: CONSONANTS

Help! The words got all mixed up.
Write the words for the pictures.

seven **ring** **picture** **lion** **wagon** **rabbit**

1. ngir

2. ieurtpc

3. ionl

4. nevse

5. gonaw

6. bitbar

REVIEW: CONSONANTS

Write the missing letters for the animals' names.

1. _____ear

2. _____at

3. _____og

4. _____ish

5. _____oat

6. _____orse

7. _____aguar

8. _____angaroo

9. _____ion

10. _____ouse

11. _____ightingale

12. _____ig

13. _____uail

14. _____abbit

15. _____eal

16. _____iger

17. _____ulture

18. _____alrus

19. fo_____

20. _____ak

21. _____ebra

Write the **beginning sounds**.
Use these letters: **n**, **q**, **s**, **y**.

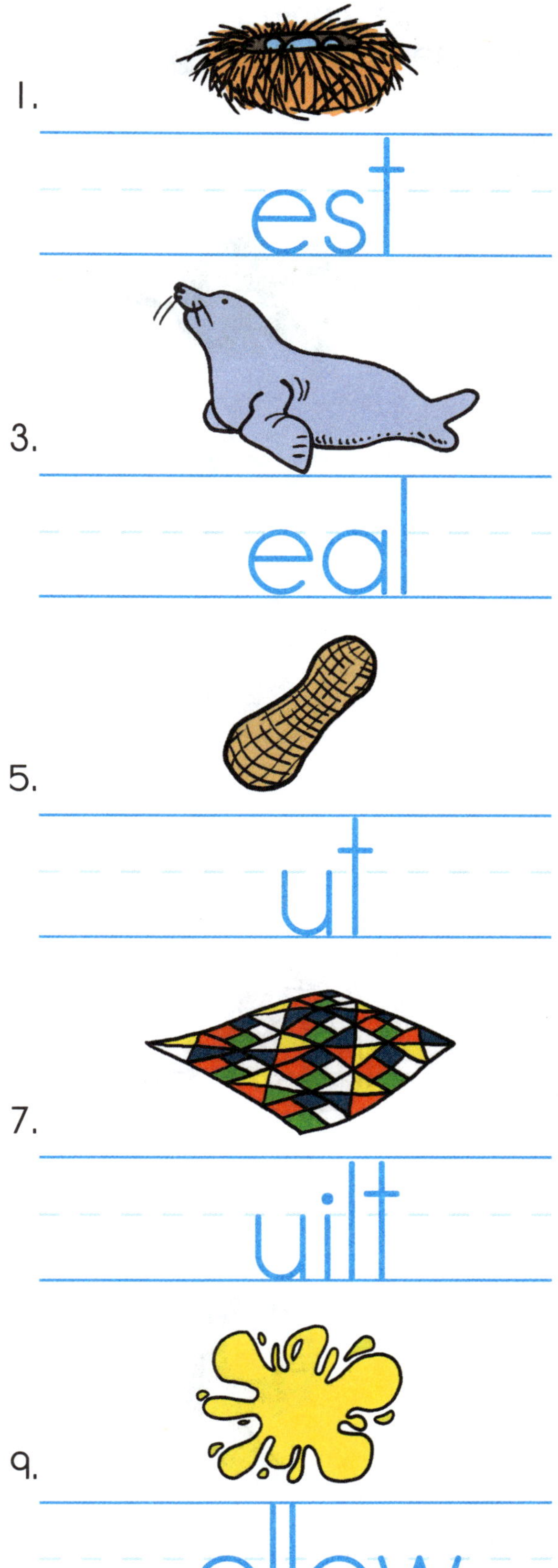

1. ___est

2. ___uail

3. ___eal

4. ___un

5. ___ut

6. ___ock

7. ___uilt

8. ___ak

9. ___ellow

Write the **beginning sounds**.
Use these letters: **b**, **d**, **g**, **l**, **n**, **q**, **s**, **y**.

1. eaf
2. og
3. all
4. ueen
5. arn
6. oat
7. ine
8. oap

BEGINNING SOUNDS

Write the **beginning sounds**.
Use these letters: **b**, **d**, **g**, **l**.

1. ___aby

2. ___og

3. ___amp

4. ___oat

5. Write a word that **begins** with **b**.

6. Write a word that **begins** with **d**.

7. Write a word that **begins** with **g**.

8. Write a word that **begins** with **l**.

Write the **beginning sounds**.
Use these letters: **c**, **f**, **h**, **k**, **m**, **p**, **r**, **t**.

Write the **beginning sounds**.
Use these letters: **c**, **f**, **h**, **k**.

Finish the words by filling in the missing letters.
Each word **begins** with the same sound as the picture.

Write the **beginning sounds**.
Use these letters: **m**, **p**, **r**, **t**.

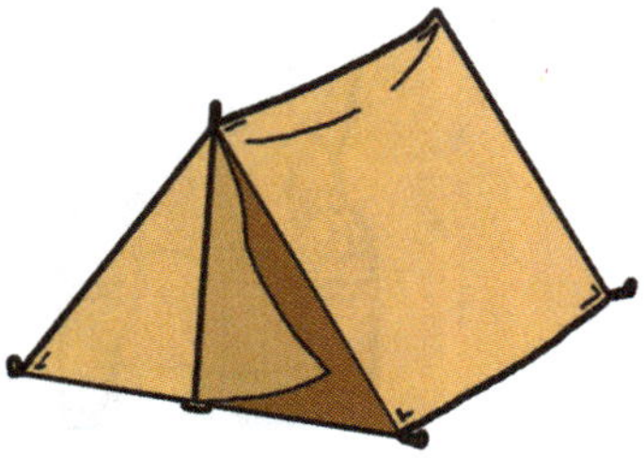

1. ent

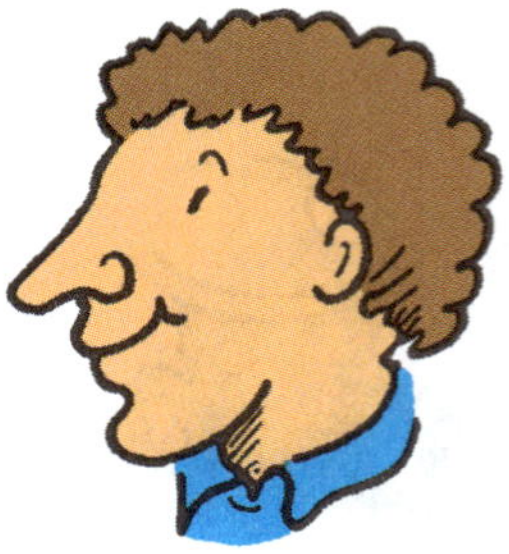

2. an

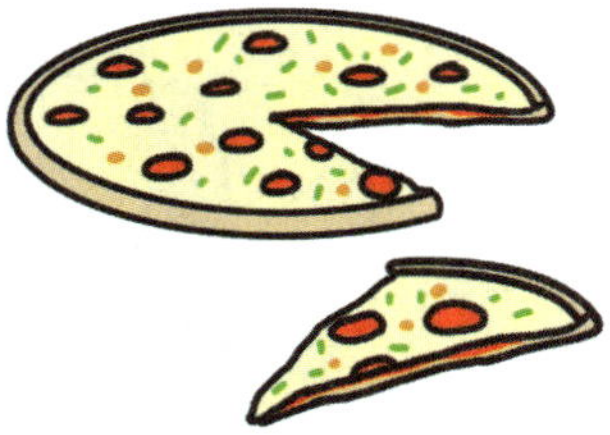

3. izza

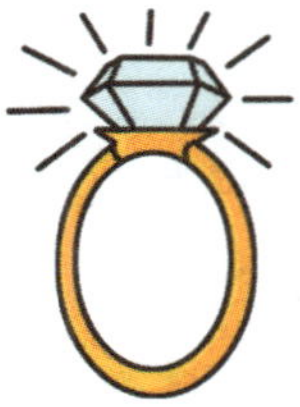

4. ing

5. Draw lines from the pictures to the letters that **begin** their names.

t

r

p

m

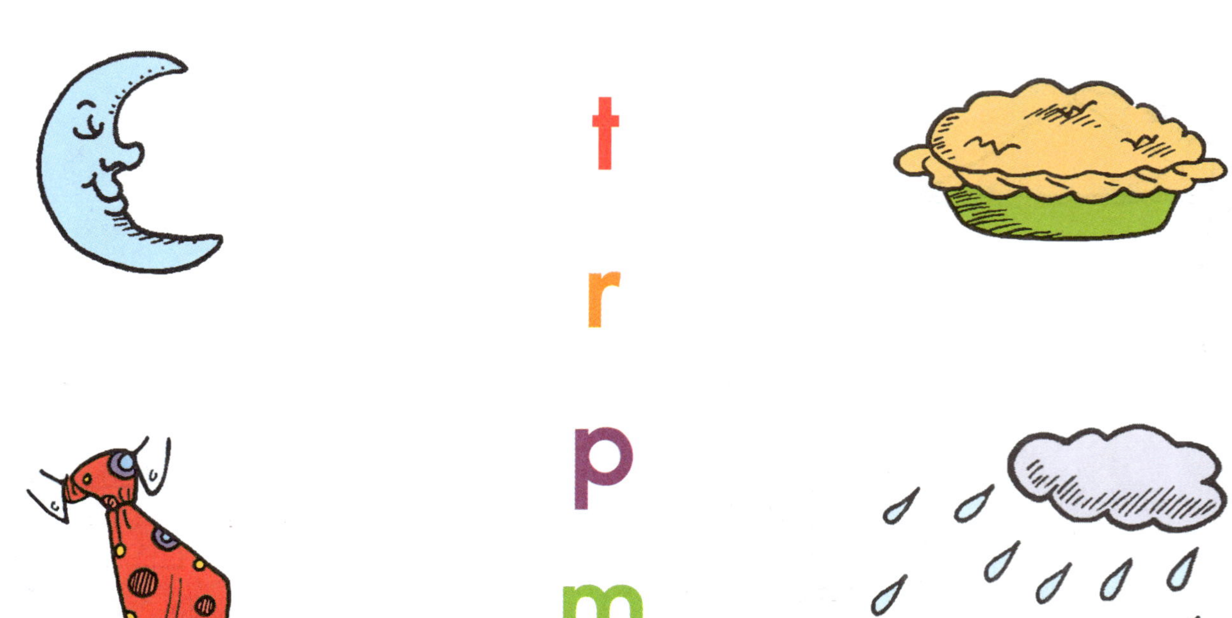

Write the **ending sounds**.
Use these letters: **b**, **g**, **l**, **m**, **n**, **p**, **r**, **x**.

Write the **ending sounds**.
Use these letters: **d**, **m**, **n**, **t**.

1. boa

2. su

3. bir

4. gu

5. Write a word that **ends** with **d**.

6. Write a word that **ends** with **t**.

7. Write a word that **ends** with **n**.

8. Write a word that **ends** with **m**.

ENDING SOUNDS

Write the **ending sounds**.
Use these letters: **d, f, k, l, o, r, s, t.**

1. re
2. sea
3. ca
4. el
5. zer
6. bu
7. ca
8. boo

Write the **ending sounds**.
Use these letters: **b**, **g**, **p**, **r**.

5. Draw lines from the pictures to the letters that **end** their names.

g

p

r

b

Write the **ending sounds**.
Use these letters: **l**, **s**, **t**, **k**.

1. 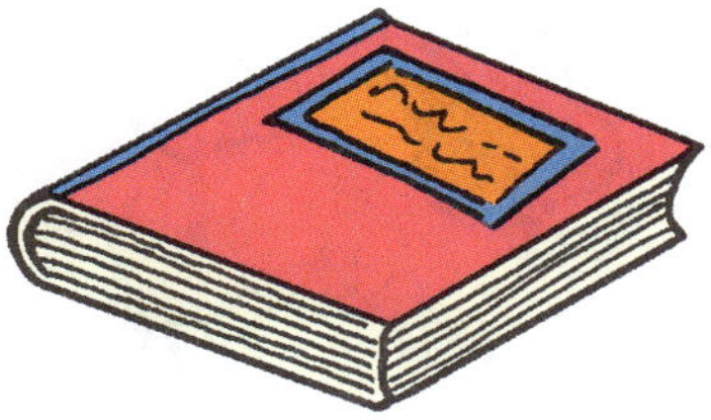 boo

2. 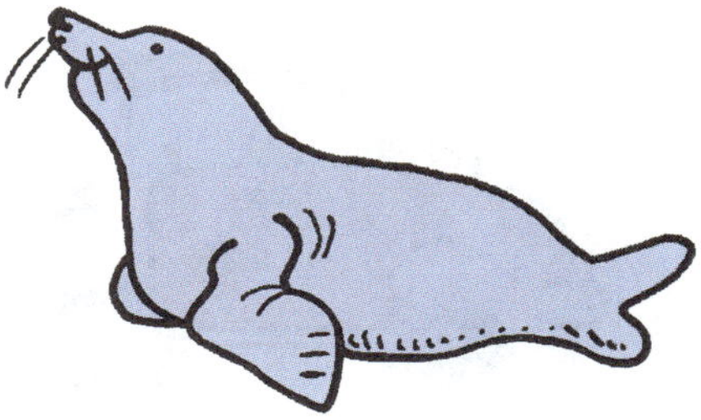 sea

3. 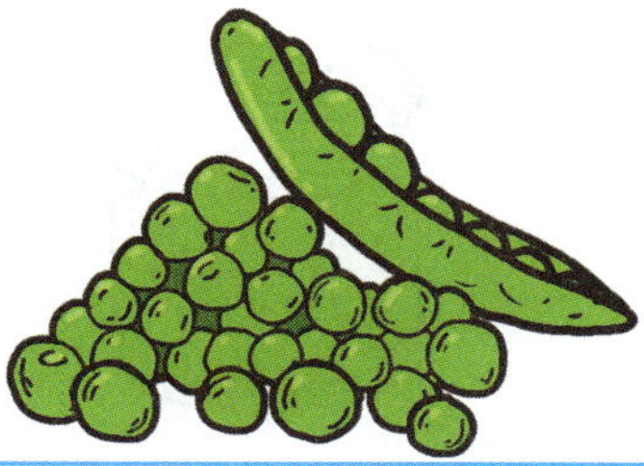 pea

4. 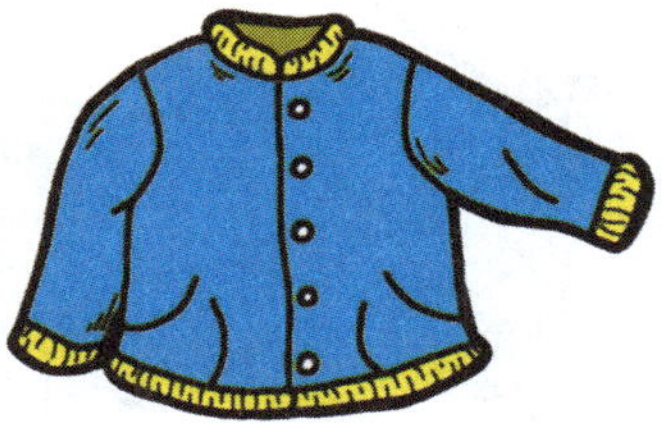 coa

Finish the words by filling in the missing letters.
Each word **ends** with the same sound as the picture.

Write the **beginning** and **ending sounds**.
Use these letters: **b**, **c**, **d**, **f**, **j**, **m**, **r**, **x**.

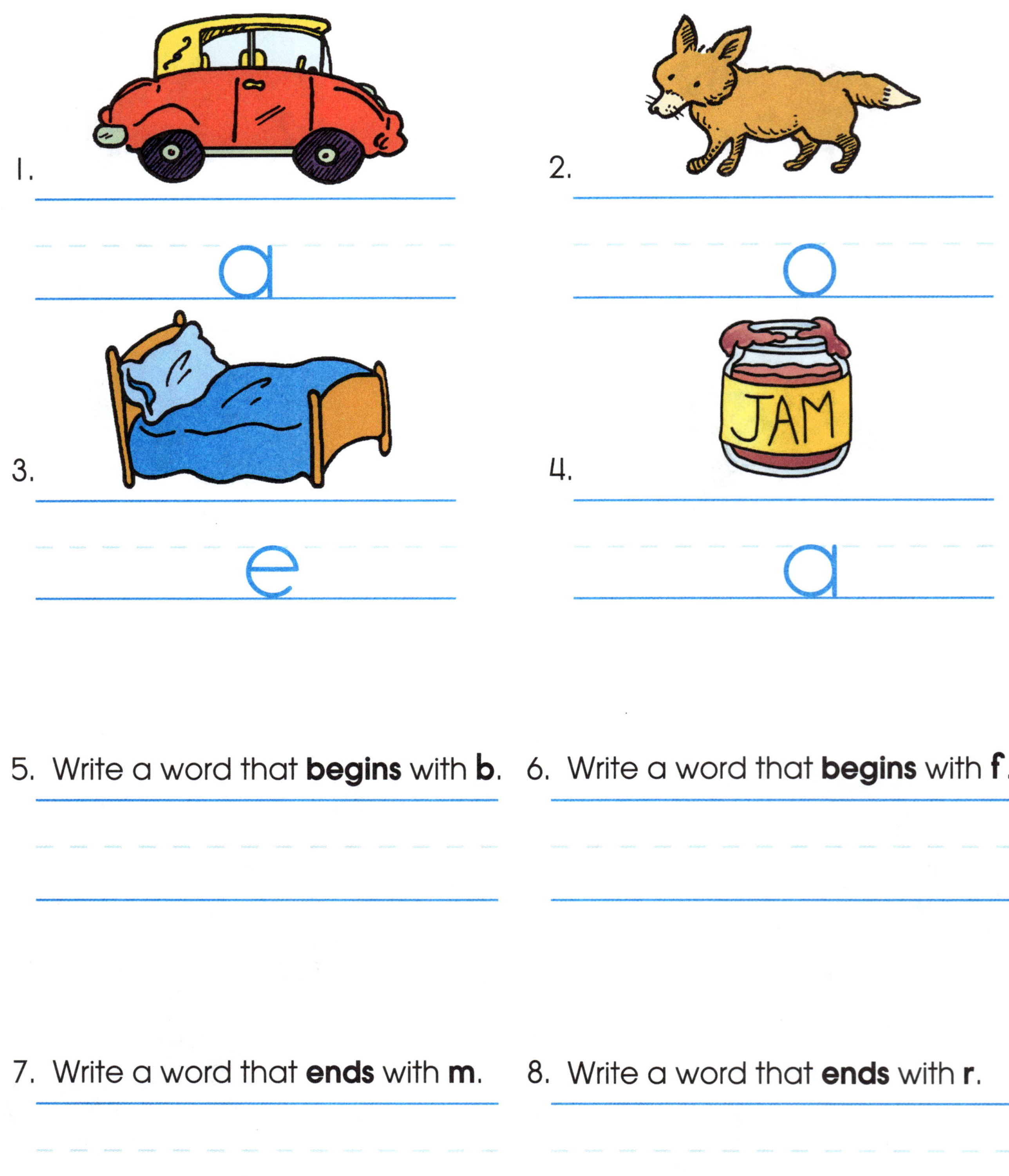

5. Write a word that **begins** with **b**.

6. Write a word that **begins** with **f**.

7. Write a word that **ends** with **m**.

8. Write a word that **ends** with **r**.

Write the **beginning** and **ending sounds**.
Use these letters: **b**, **g**, **m**, **n**, **p**, **s**, **t**.

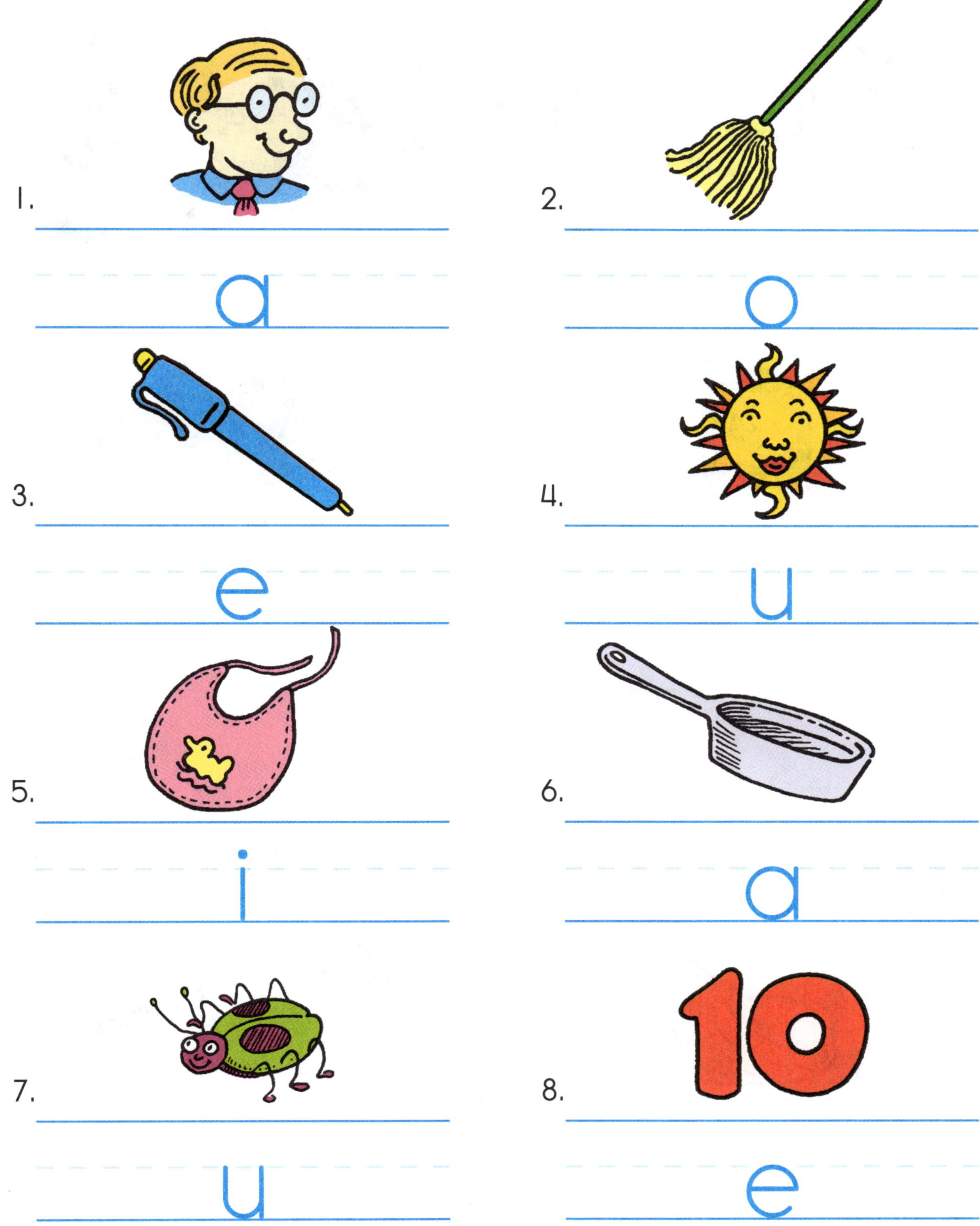

WORDS WITH SHORT a

These words have the **short a** sound in .

pan cat
fan nap
dad bat

Write the **short a** words that **rhyme** with the pictures.

1.

2.

Write the **short a** words that **begin** with the same letters as the pictures.

3.

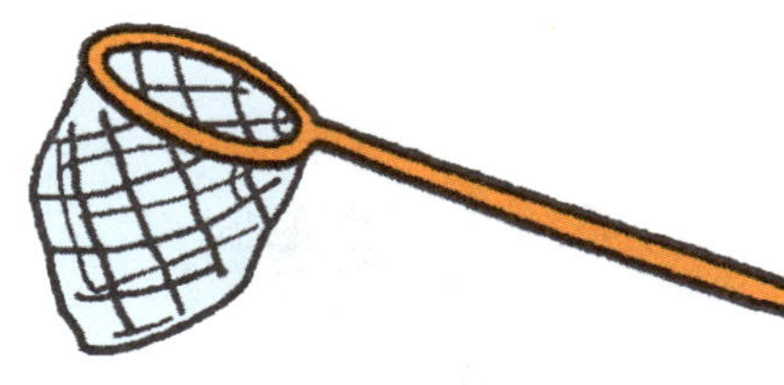

4.

WORDS WITH SHORT a

Write the **short a** words for the pictures.

man bag cat map

1.

2.

3.

4.

Write the **short a** words that **begin** with the same letters as the pictures.

5.

6.

1. Color the **short a** words blue.

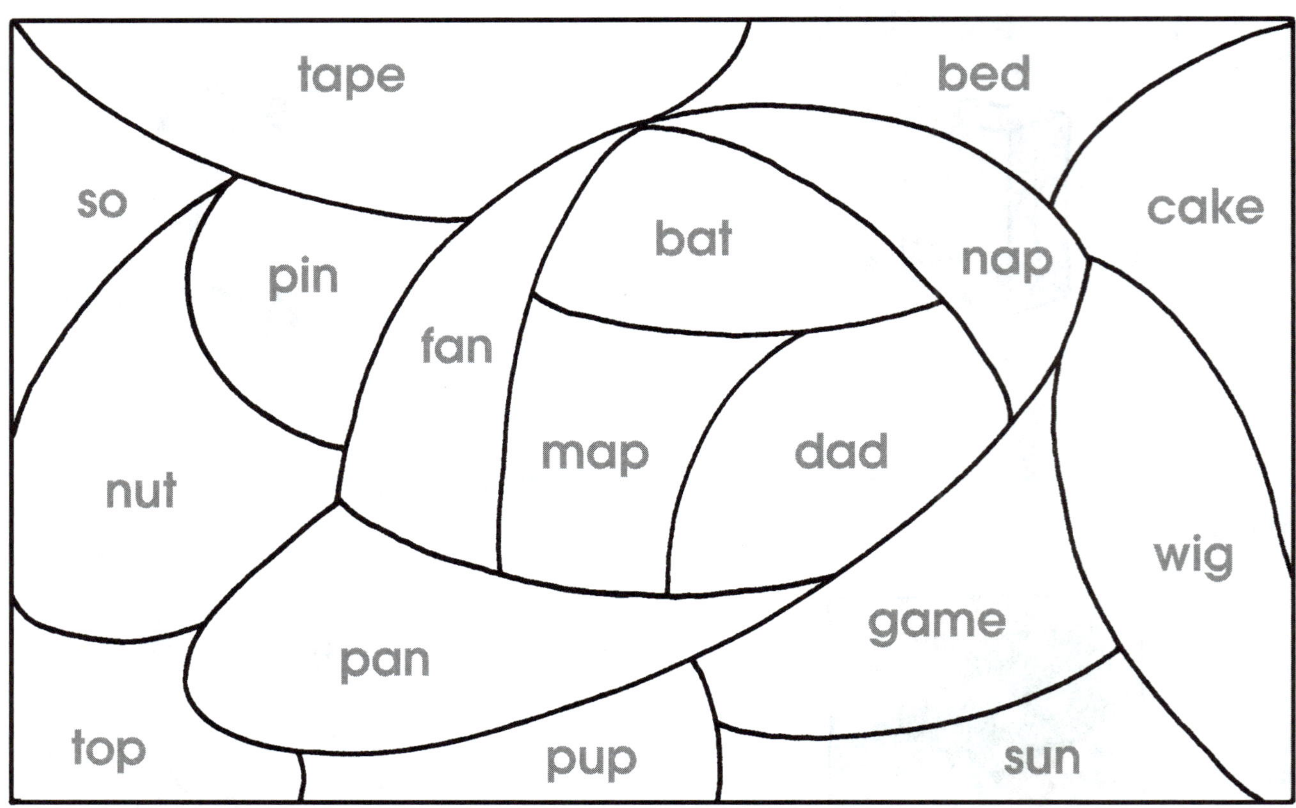

2. Write the **short a** words.

1. Color the balloons that have **short a** words yellow.

map
stay
fan
star
hat
bag
can
sat
play
snake
cake
game

2. Add the letters **b**, **m**, **p**, and **r** to make **short a** words.

Write the **short a** words for the pictures.

van bat cat fan stamp lamp mask tack

1. 

2.

3. 

4.

5. 

6. 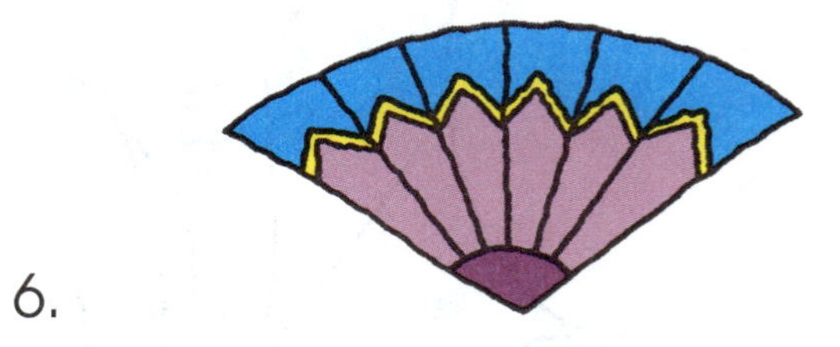

7. 

8. 

WORDS WITH SHORT a

Write the **short a** words to finish the sentences.

cat
tag
bat
hand
mask

1. PAT: Let's play baseball. I'll get the ball and _____ .

2. SALLY: If I want to be the catcher, I'll need to wear a_____.

3. SALLY: My_____will be our mascot.

4. PAT: I can catch the ball with my mitt on my_____.

5. SALLY: I will_____runners to get the winning out!

1. Color the **short a** words **red**.

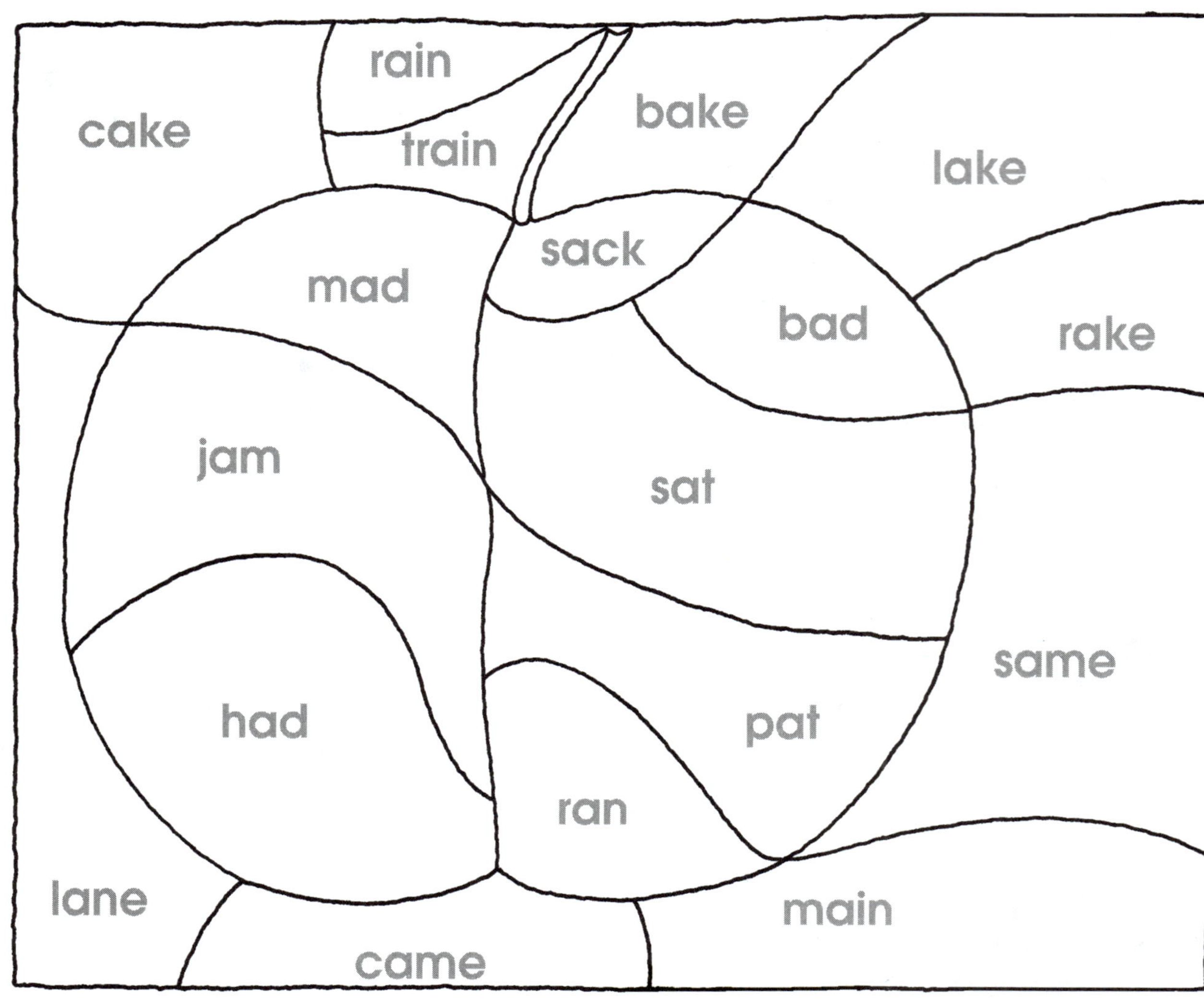

2. Write the **short a** words.

WORDS WITH SHORT a

had can sat dad ran bat

1. Write the **short a** words that **rhyme** with **bad**.

2. Write the **short a** words that **rhyme** with **fan**.

3. Write the **short a** words that **rhyme** with **hat**.

Write the **short a** words to finish the sentences.

4. My____________ has a new car.

5. Joe took his ball and ____________ with him.

6. Mother said I ____________ go to the game.

7. The dog ____________ away with the bone.

8. I don't know who ____________ on the bed.

9. Jill ____________ a cold and could not go.

WORDS WITH SHORT a

at as cat fan am ant an had

1. Write the **short a** words that have two letters.

2. Write the **short a** words that have three letters.

Spell **short a** words by adding the **short a** endings.

3. **at**	4. **am**	5. **an**	6. **ad**
b ___ ___	h ___ ___	r ___ ___	b ___ ___
h ___ ___	j ___ ___	m ___ ___	d ___ ___
m ___ ___	S ___ ___	p ___ ___	h ___ ___
p ___ ___	r ___ ___	f ___ ___	m ___ ___

Write the **short a** words for the pictures.

fan bat pan hat

1.

2.

3.

4.

5. Add **ad** to make **short a** words.

m

s

6. Add **an** to make **short a** words.

r

c

WORDS WITH SHORT a

1. Color the **short a** words orange.

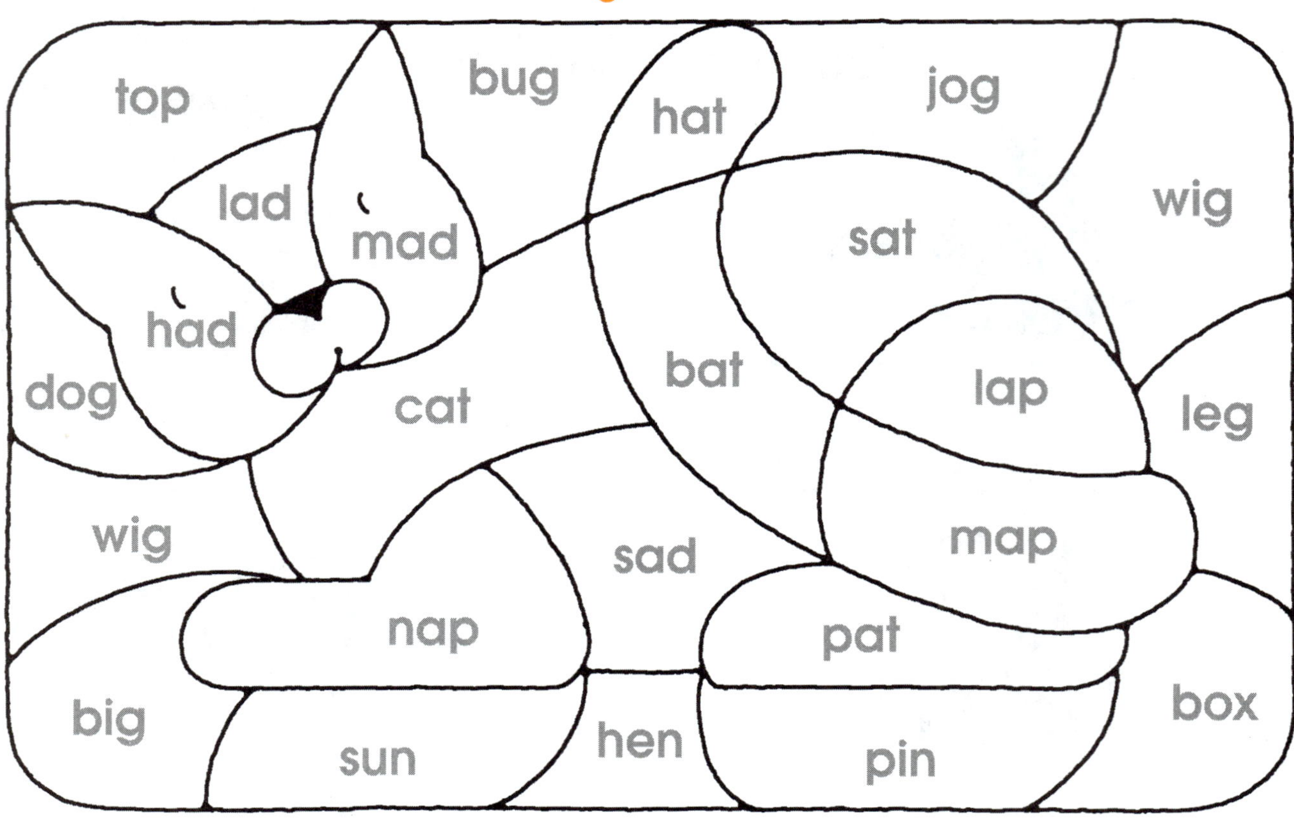

2. Add **at** to make **short a** words.

c

s

h

3. Add **ap** to make **short a** words.

n

l

m

These words have the **short e** sound in 

pen **ten** **bell**
net **pet** **bed**

Write the **short e** words that fit the shapes.

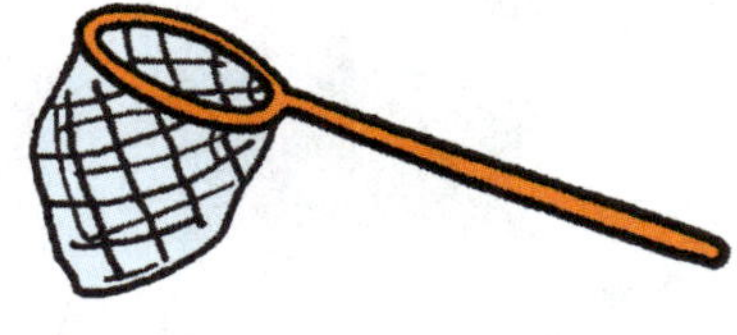

1. 

2. 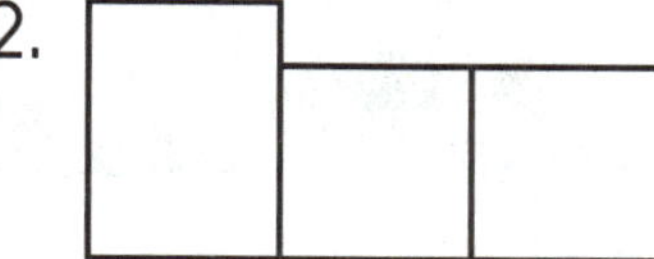

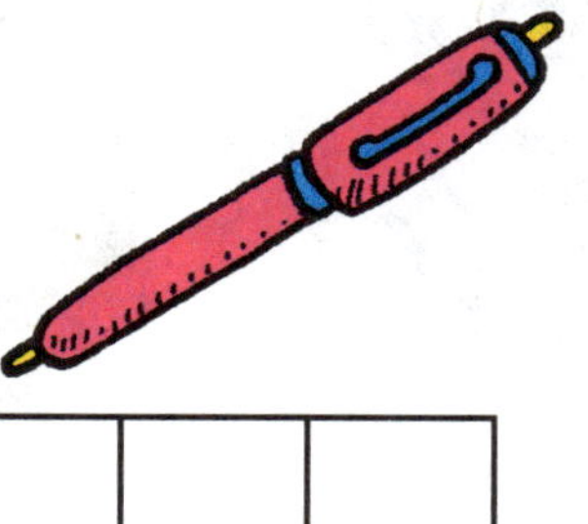

3.

4. 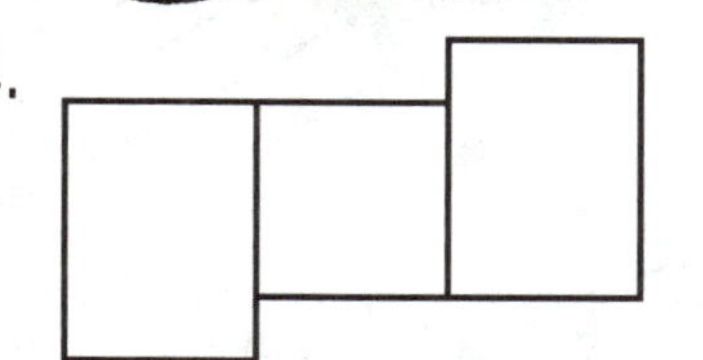

Write the **short e** words for the pictures.

5. ______________________

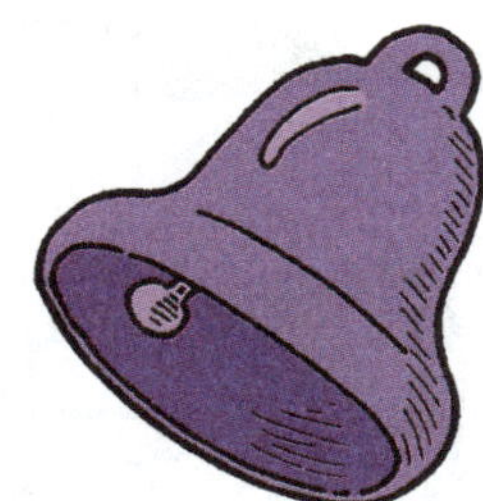

6. ______________________

Help Elmer Elephant get to his playhouse.
Write the **short e** words by the pictures.

tent sled ten
nest bell bed

men red ten let bed get

1. Write the **short e** words that **end** with **n**.

2. Write the **short e** words that **rhyme** with **pet**.

3. Write the **short e** words that **end** with **d**.

Write the **short e** words to finish the sentences.

4. Mary has a new ____________ dress.

5. Sam will be ____________ on his birthday.

6. What did Sam ____________ from his grandmother?

7. Our dog sleeps on his own ____________.

8. We ____________ our cat sleep with us.

9. How many ____________ are in the band?

Circle the **short e** words in the word search.

when smell best end send lend
tent cent deck tell get wet

W	H	E	N	Z	R	X	T	S
O	S	N	F	G	S	E	N	D
H	M	D	Q	T	D	Z	N	G
T	E	N	T	W	E	W	T	E
P	L	V	X	T	C	E	N	T
B	L	D	Z	M	K	T	E	L
T	L	E	N	D	U	O	Q	Z
K	T	Q	T	E	L	L	H	P
B	E	S	T	C	B	A	V	D

WORDS WITH SHORT e

Draw lines from the **short e** words to their pictures.
Then write the **short e** words under the pictures.

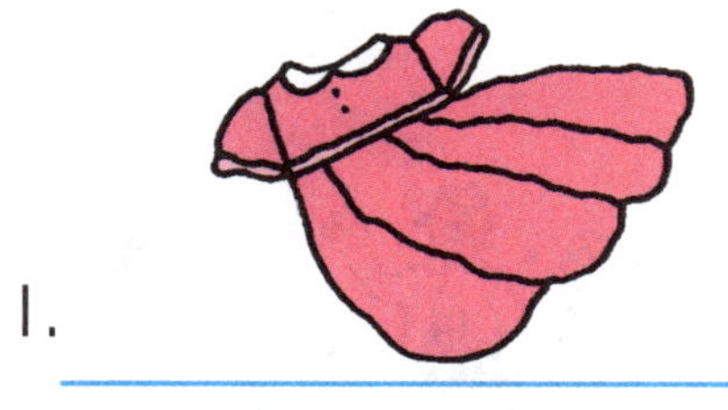

1.

web

2.

belt

3.

pen

4.

dress

5.

desk

hen

6.

7.

bed

WORDS WITH SHORT e

Write the **short e** words that fit the shapes.

bed men ten web jet red get bell

1.

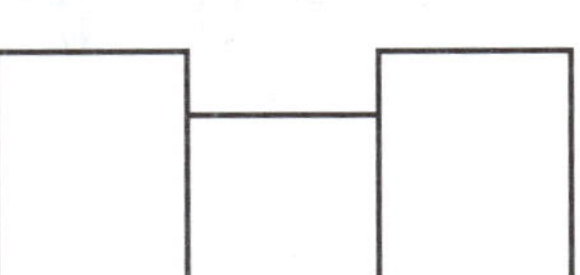

2.

3.

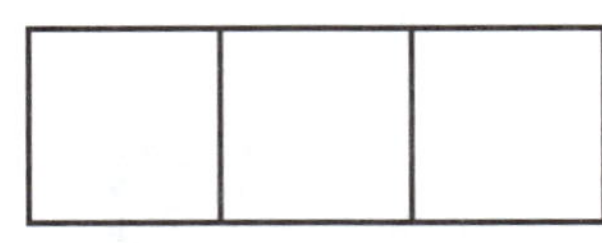

4.

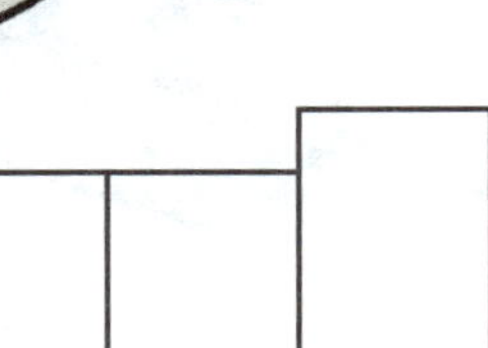

5.

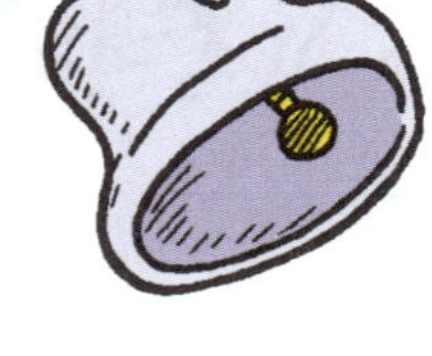

6.

7. Write the **short e** words that **rhyme** with **met**.

8. Write the **short e** words that **rhyme** with **hen**.

9. Write the **short e** words that **rhyme** with **fed**.

WORDS WITH SHORT e

1. Color the **short e** words **red**.

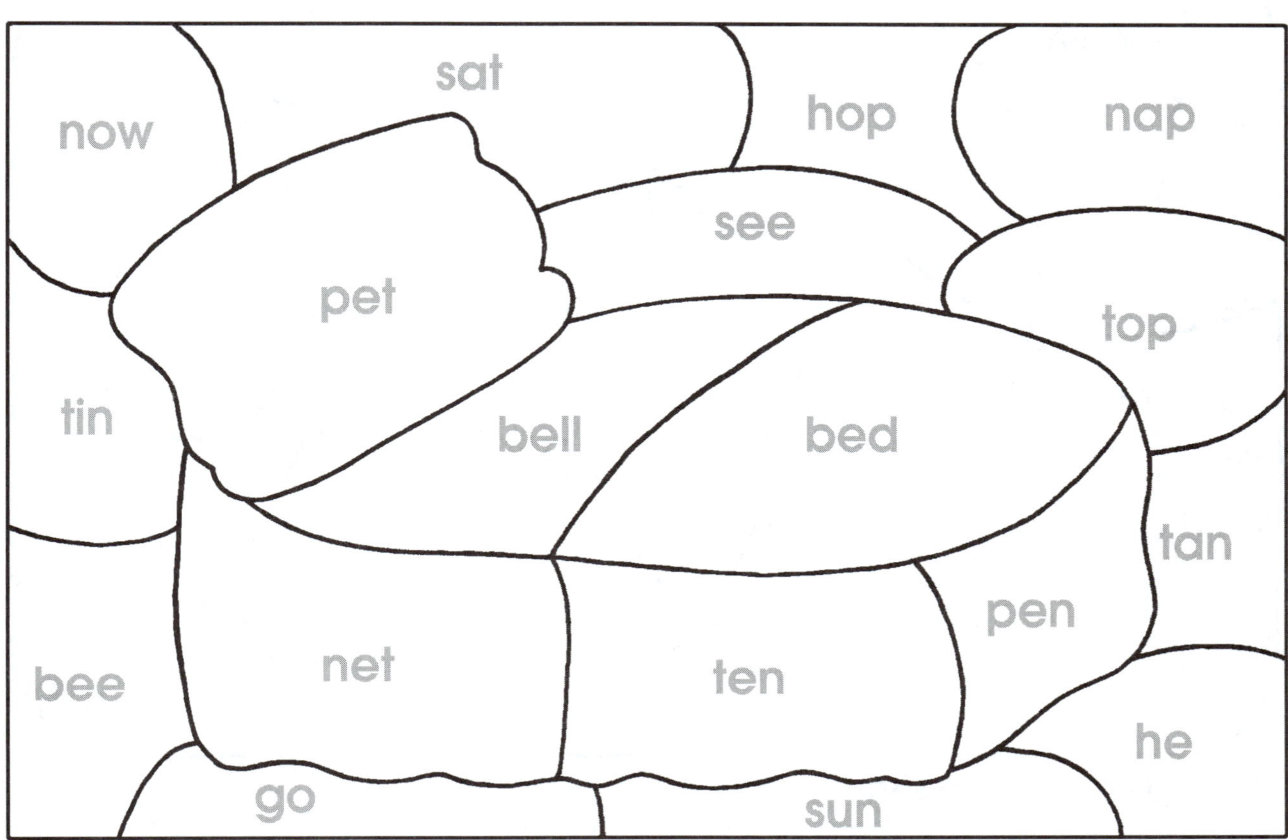

2. Write the **short e** words.

1. Color the **short e** words **blue**.

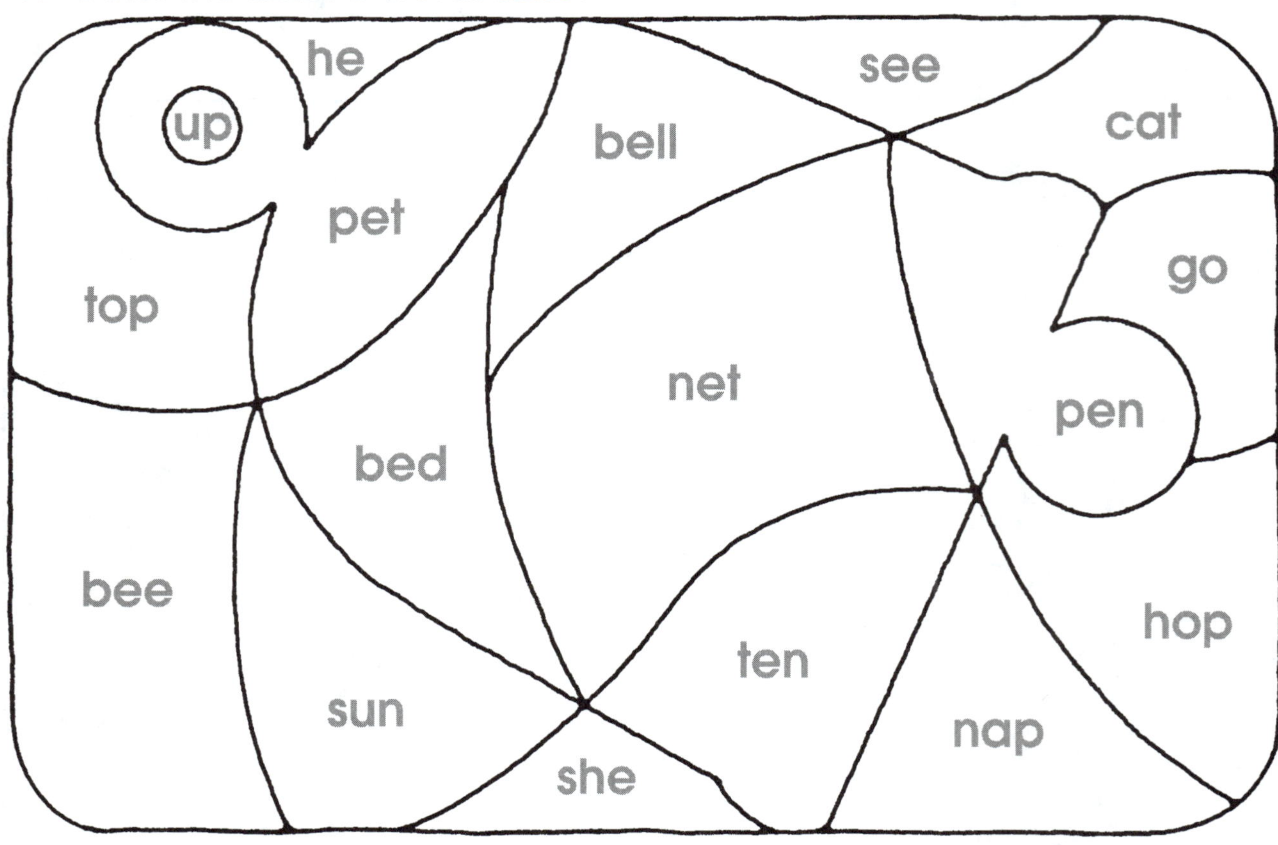

2. Add **et** to make **short e** words.

g

w

p

3. Add **en** to make **short e** words.

t

p

h

1. Help the girl find her pet.
   Follow the path of **short e** words.

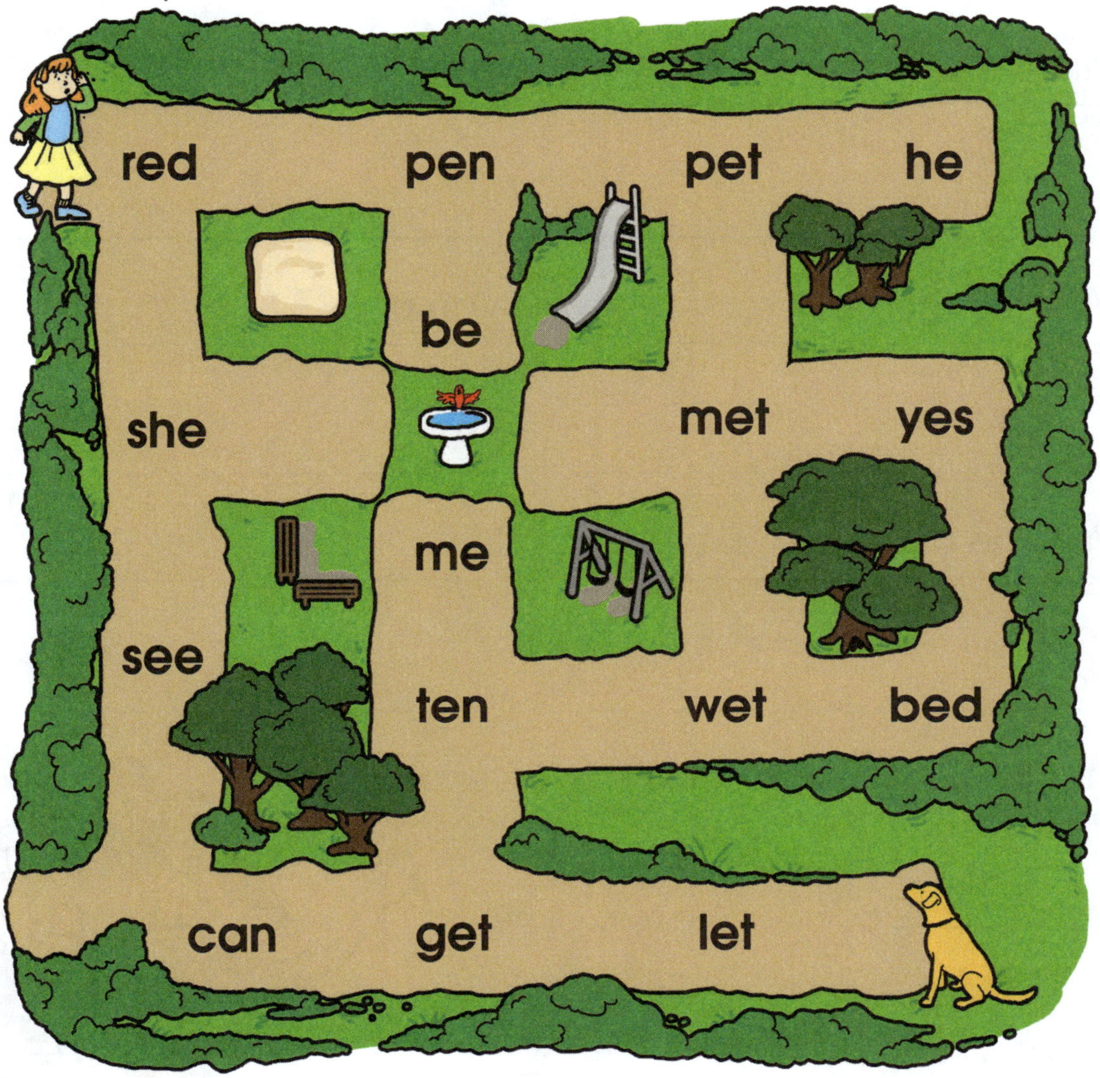
red
pen
pet
he
be
she
met
yes
me
see
ten
wet
bed
can
get
let

2. Write the **short e** words that **rhyme** with **men**.

3. Add the letter **b** to make **short e** words.

___et ___ed

4. Add the letter **l** to make **short e** words.

___et ___ed

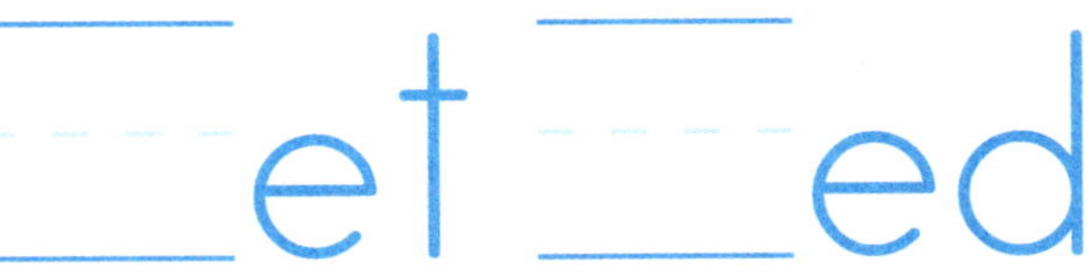

WORDS WITH SHORT e

let   bed   get   men   red   ten

1. Write the **short e** words that **end** with **n**.

2. Write the **short e** words that **rhyme** with **pet**.

3. Write the **short e** words that **end** with **d**.

Write the **short e** words to finish the sentences.

4. ____________ pennies make a dime.

5. Our dog sleeps on my ____________ .

6. What did you ____________ for your birthday?

7. The ____________ worked late today.

8. Dad has a ____________ truck.

9. Will your mother ____________ you come?

Write the **short e** answers to the riddles.

ten	cent	belt	hen	bell	pen
red	sled	tent	nest	bed	desk

1. We ride on it when there is snow. ______________
2. We write with it. ______________
3. We can sleep in it outdoors. ______________
4. It makes a ringing sound. ______________
5. Fire trucks are often this color. ______________
6. A dime is this many pennies. ______________
7. It lays eggs. ______________
8. We sit at one in school. ______________
9. It holds up your pants. ______________
10. We sleep on it. ______________
11. A penny is one. ______________
12. Baby birds stay in it. ______________

WORDS WITH SHORT a & e

Write the correct **short vowel a** or **e** on the lines.
Draw lines from the **short a** and **e** words to their pictures.

1. w ___ b

2. f ___ n

3. ___ pple

4. ___ nt

5. sl ___ d

6. t ___ nt

7. d ___ sk

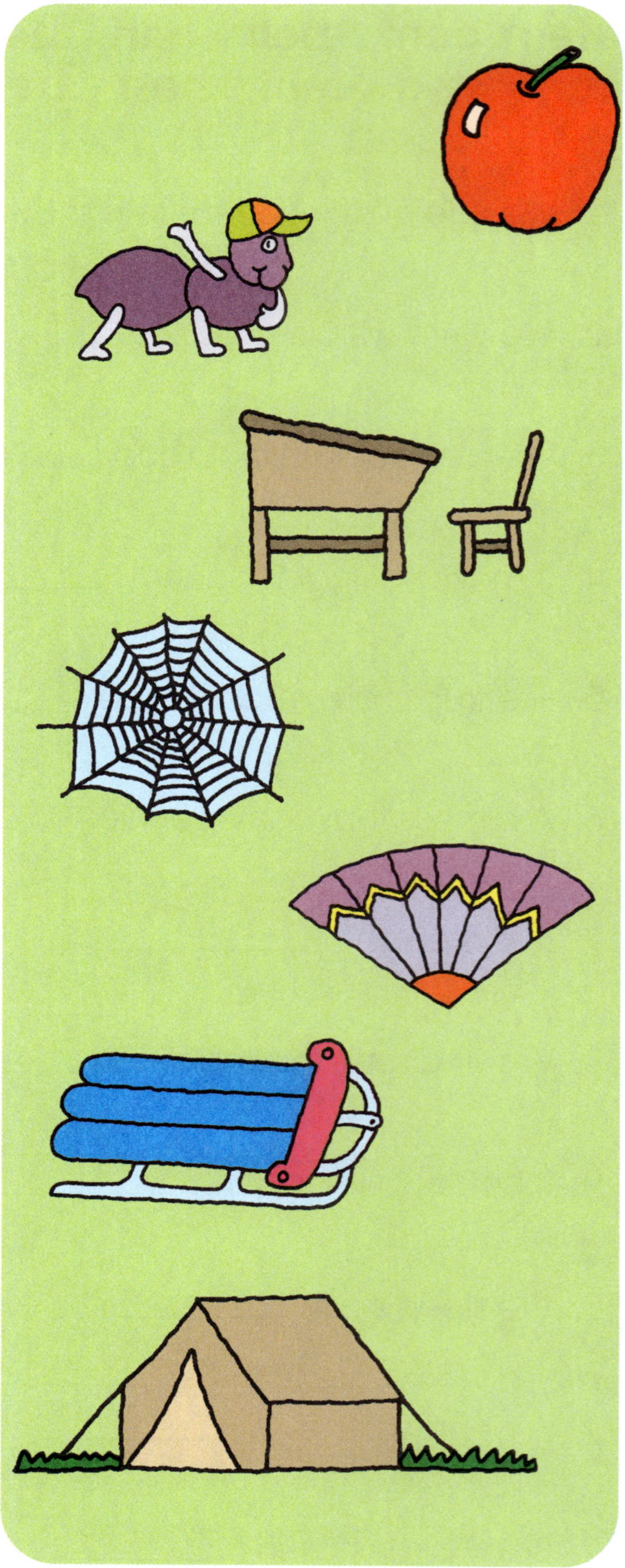

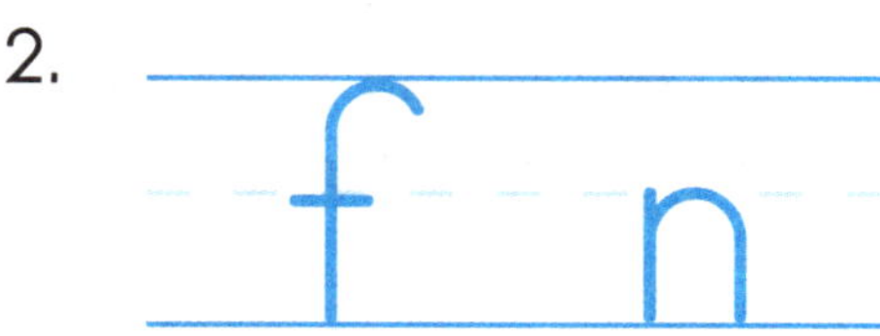

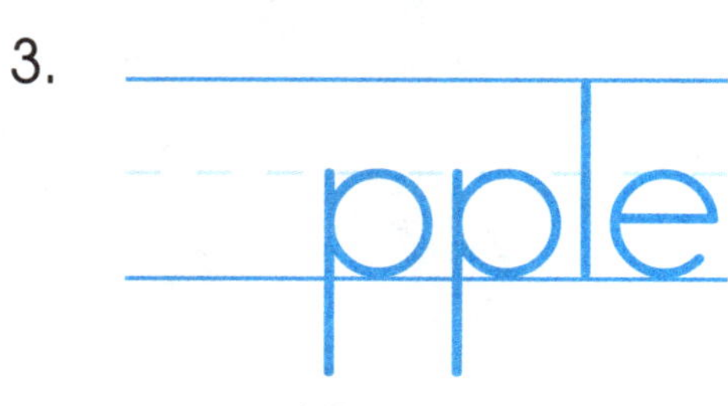

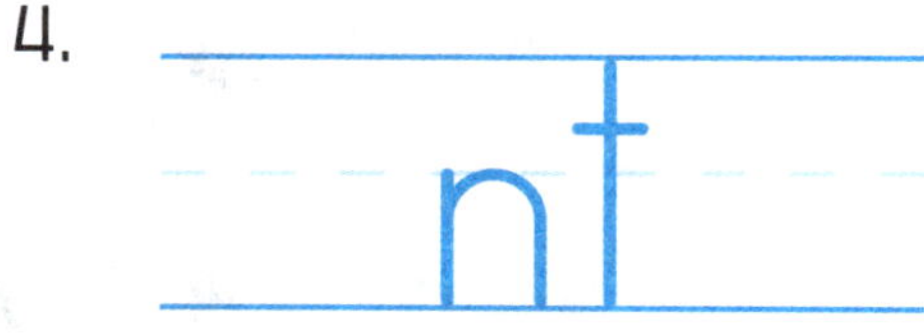

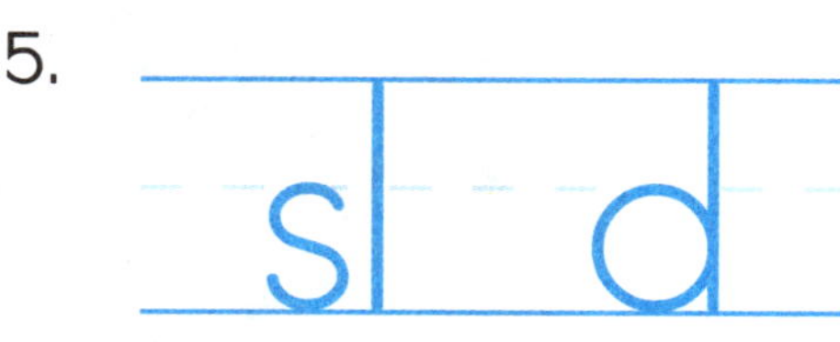

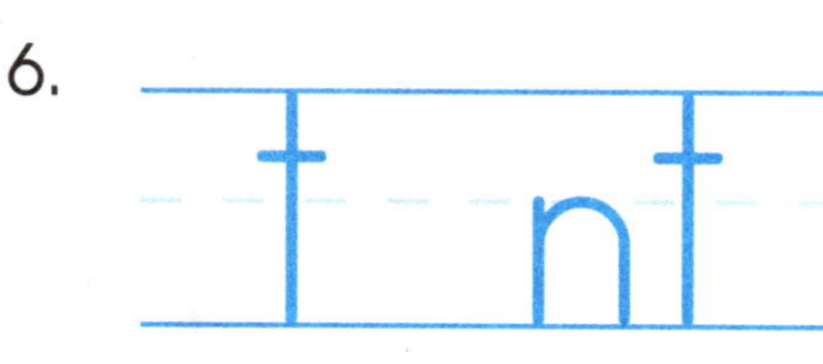

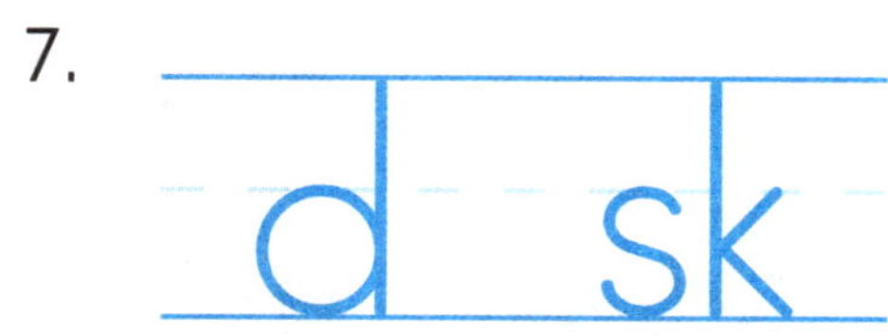

These words have the **short i** sound in .

big dig in
pig wig his

Write the **short i** words that mean the **opposite** of:

1.

out

2.

hers

3. Write the **short i** words that **end** with **ig**.

WORDS WITH SHORT i

Write the **short i** words that fit the shapes.

six sit fish big pig did give his

1. 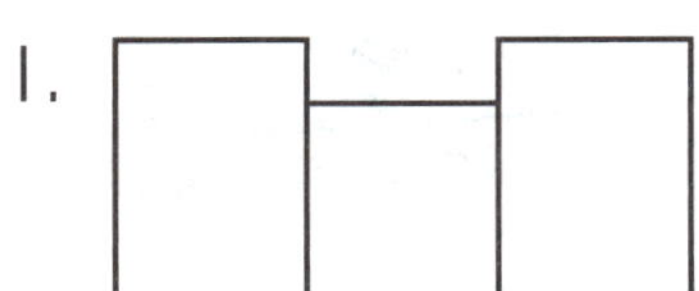

2.

3.

4. 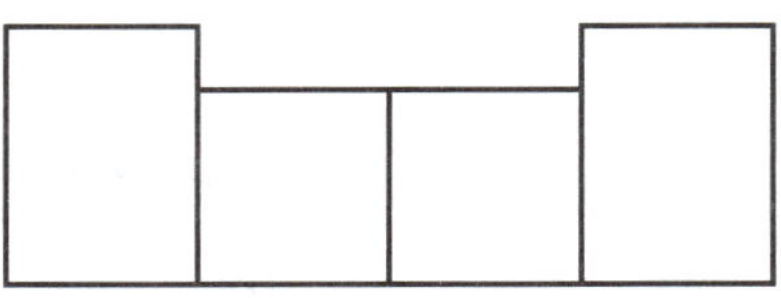

5.

6.

7.

8. 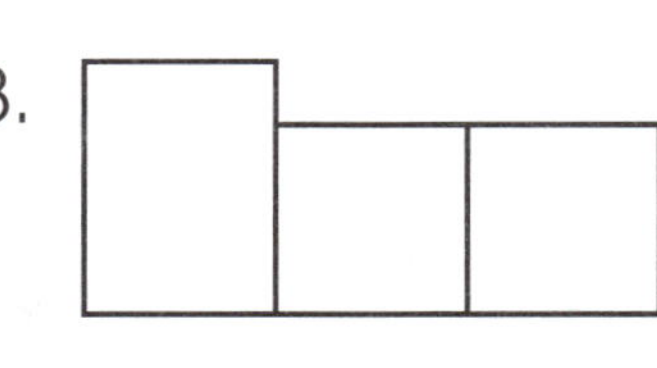

Write the **short i** words that **rhyme** with:

9. **big** ________

10. **fix** ________

11. **live** ________

12. **hit** ________

13. **dish** ________

14. **hid** 

1. Color the **short i** words pink.

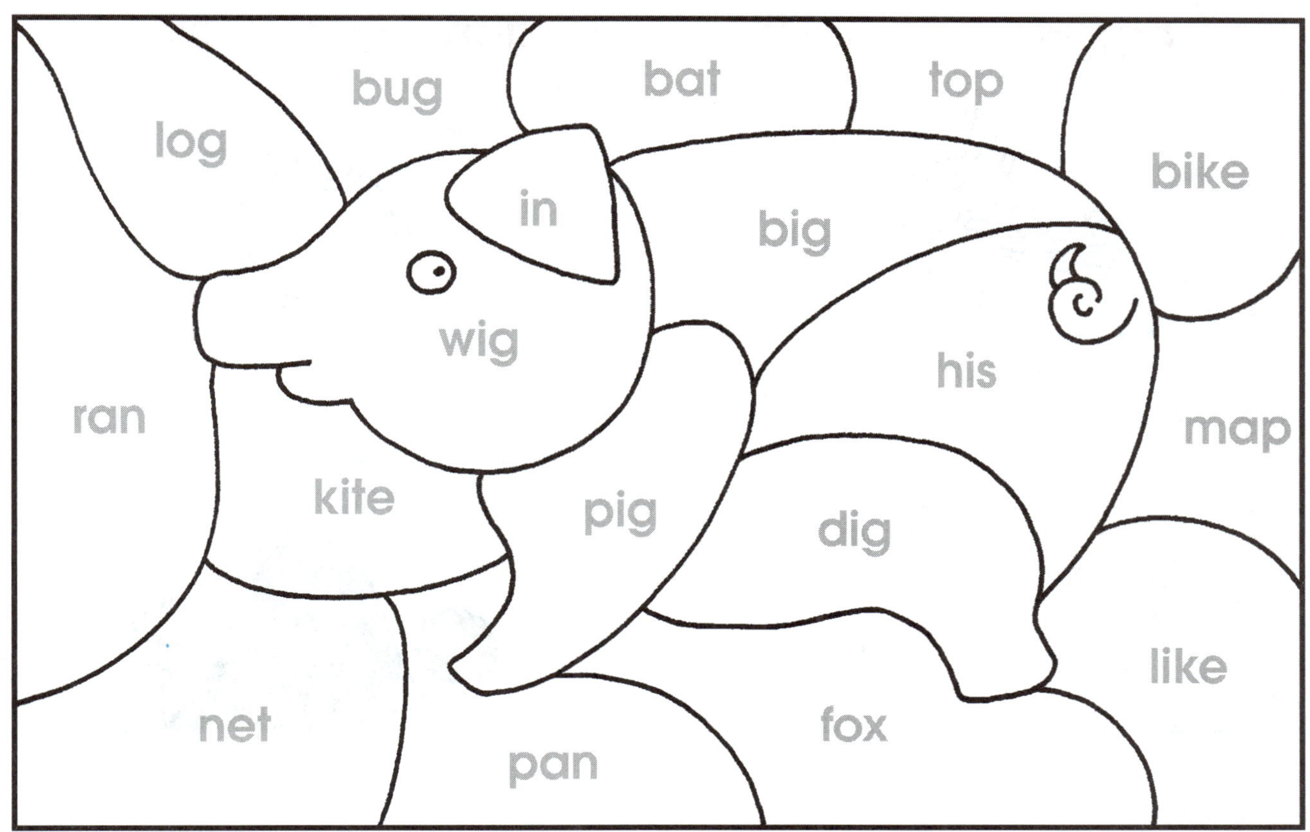

2. Write the **short i** words.

WORDS WITH SHORT i

Write the **short i** words for the pictures.

pig gift fish hill wig dish brick bib

1.

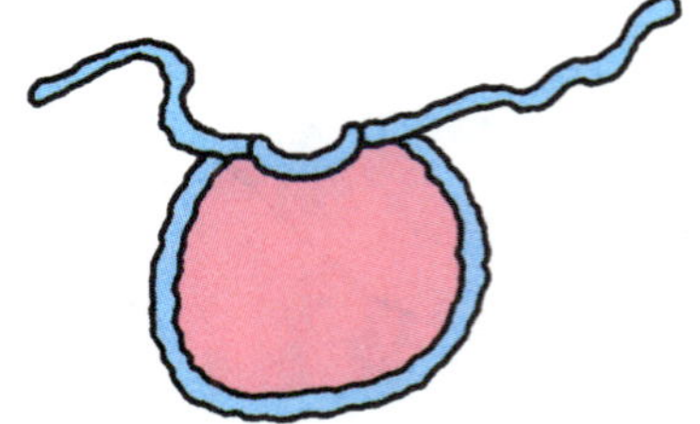

2.

3.

4.

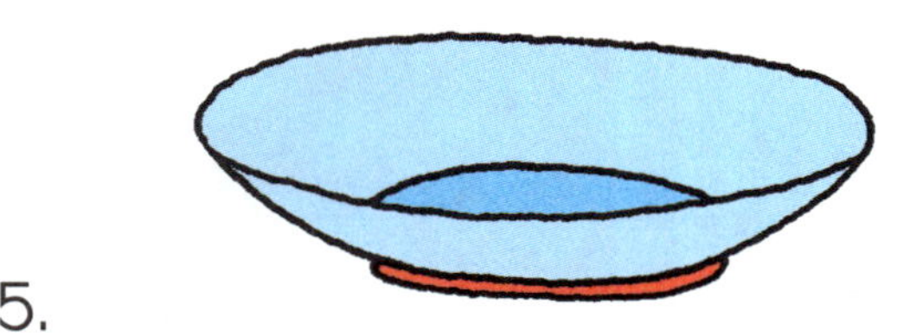

5.

6.

7.

8.

WORDS WITH SHORT i

Write the **short i** words to finish the sentences.

it **sit** **six** **quit** **win** **hits** **miss** **begin**

1. The game begins at____________.

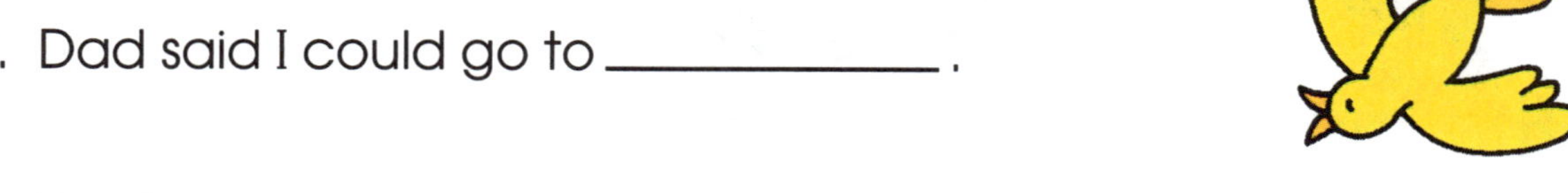

2. Dad said I could go to ____________.

3. We found a place to ____________.

4. We saw batters make ____________.

5. Sometimes they would ____________.

6. But they will never____________.

7. Each team wants to ____________.

8. Then new games will ____________.

9. Draw lines between the **rhyming short i** words.

fish	**hit**
pig	**fix**
win	**big**
sit	**pin**
six	**dish**

WORDS WITH SHORT i

Circle the correct spellings for the **short i** pictures.

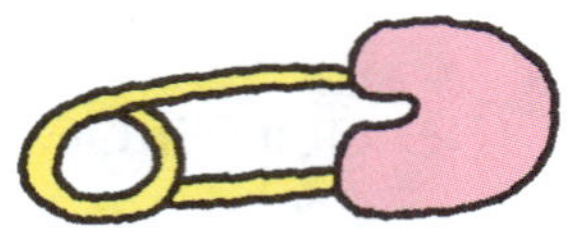

1. **fich** **fish**
2. **ring** **ringh**
3. **pin** **pinn**

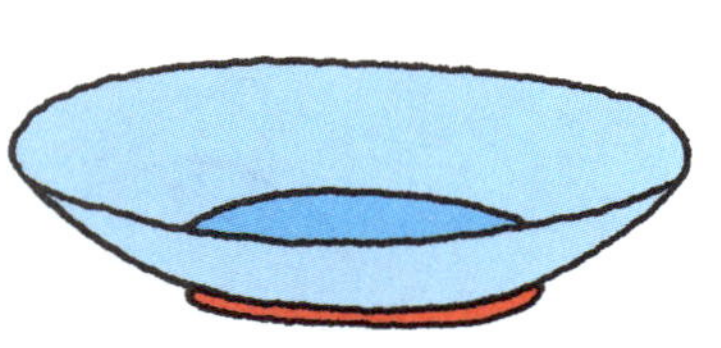

4. **dish** **dishe**
5. **hill** **hile**
6. **bieb** **bib**

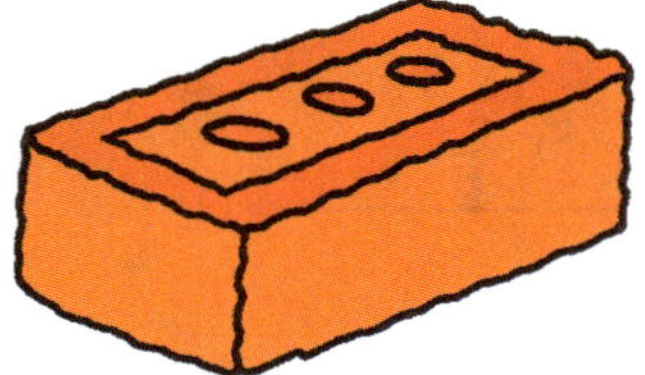
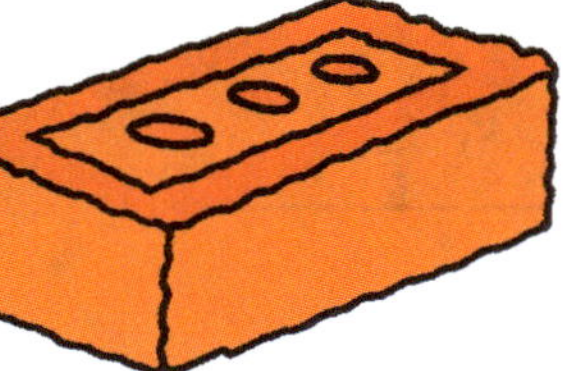

7. **six** **sis**
8. **brick** **brik**
9. **pig** **pieg**

10. **gipht** **gift**
11. **lips** **lipz**
12. **fifty** **fity**

WORDS WITH SHORT i

Write **i** in the blanks to finish the silly sentences.
Read the sentences to a friend.

1. I h___d the l___d, I d___d.

2. I w___ll f___ll the h___ll with flowers.

3. The b___g p___g ate a f___g.

4. I w___sh the f___sh were still in the d___sh.

Add the missing letters to make the **short i** words from the sentences above.

5. ___id 6. ___ill 7. ___ig 8. ___ish

___id ___ill ___ig ___ish

___id ___ill ___ig ___ish

9. Write two silly sentences that have **short i** words.

____

____

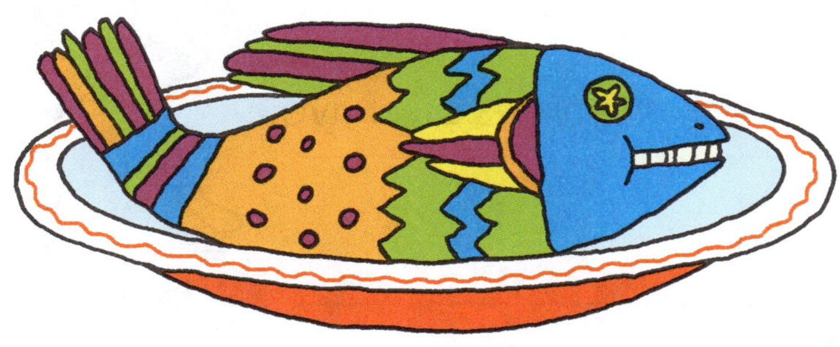

Write the **short i** words that mean the **opposite** of:

six give big pig fish his

1\. 

little

2\. 

take

3\. 

hers

Write the **short i** words for the pictures.

4\. 

5\. 

6\. Write the number that comes after five.

WORDS WITH SHORT i

1. Circle the **short i** words in the word search.

big	pig	his	fish	give	six	fire	pin
hill	little	dish	brick	hid	sit	lips	lid

L	I	T	T	L	E	F	S	P	T
J	P	G	I	V	E	I	I	O	M
Q	I	X	Z	W	S	S	X	Z	P
P	N	L	B	Z	I	H	M	H	I
T	F	I	R	E	T	H	B	I	G
H	P	D	I	S	H	I	W	S	I
Z	Y	X	C	G	Q	L	R	T	V
W	O	I	K	D	M	L	I	P	S
H	I	D	W	P	S	Q	Z	X	C

2. Add **ig** to make **short i** words.

3. Add **ish** to make **short i** words.

WORDS WITH SHORT i

fish sick fix dish six kick

1. Write the **short i** words that **end** with **sh**.

2. Write the **short i** words that **end** with **x**.

3. Write the **short i** words that **rhyme** with **pick**.

4. Color the **short i** words **blue**.

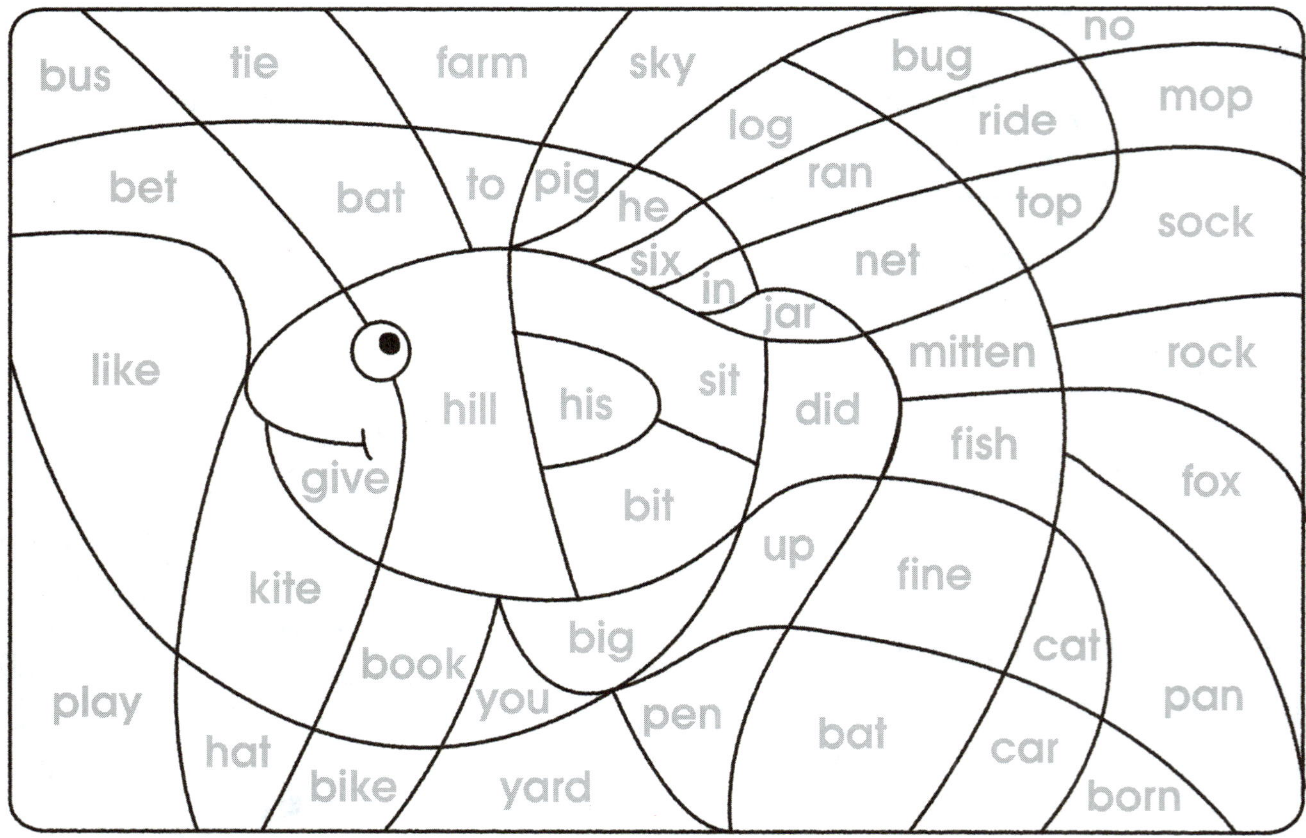

WORDS WITH SHORT i

sit six big dish dig bit his fish

1. Write the **short i** words that **rhyme** with **pig**.

2. Write the **short i** words that **rhyme** with **fit**.

3. Write the **short i** words that **rhyme** with **wish**.

Write the **short i** words to finish the sentences.

4. He lost ____________ cap.

5. Anna is ____________ years old.

WORDS WITH SHORT o

These words have the **short o** sound in octopus.

pot	not	lot
top	box	sock

Write the **short o** words for the pictures inside the shapes.

1.

2.

3.

4. Write the **short o** words that **rhyme** with **hot**.

WORDS WITH SHORT o

Write the **short o** words for the pictures.

mop **top** **box** **doll** **lock** **sock** **clock** **block**

Write the **short o** words to finish the sentences.

fox **top** **clock** **mop** **block** **box**

1. The ____________ sat on the ____________.

2. A mouse was on ____________ of the ____________.

3. I had to ____________ around the ____________.

4. Circle the **short o** words in the word search.

C	L	O	C	K	J	X	G
M	K	P	L	D	J	B	J
T	S	F	O	X	O	L	O
O	W	T	Q	N	A	O	V
P	Z	U	I	M	H	C	U
L	J	U	D	O	P	K	Y
B	O	X	C	P	H	M	C

WORDS WITH SHORT o

Write the **short o** words for the pictures.

hot doll not fox lot box

1.

2.

3. Write the **short o** words that **end** with **t**.

4. Write the **short o** word that **rhymes** with **fox**.

1. Color the **short o** words **purple**.

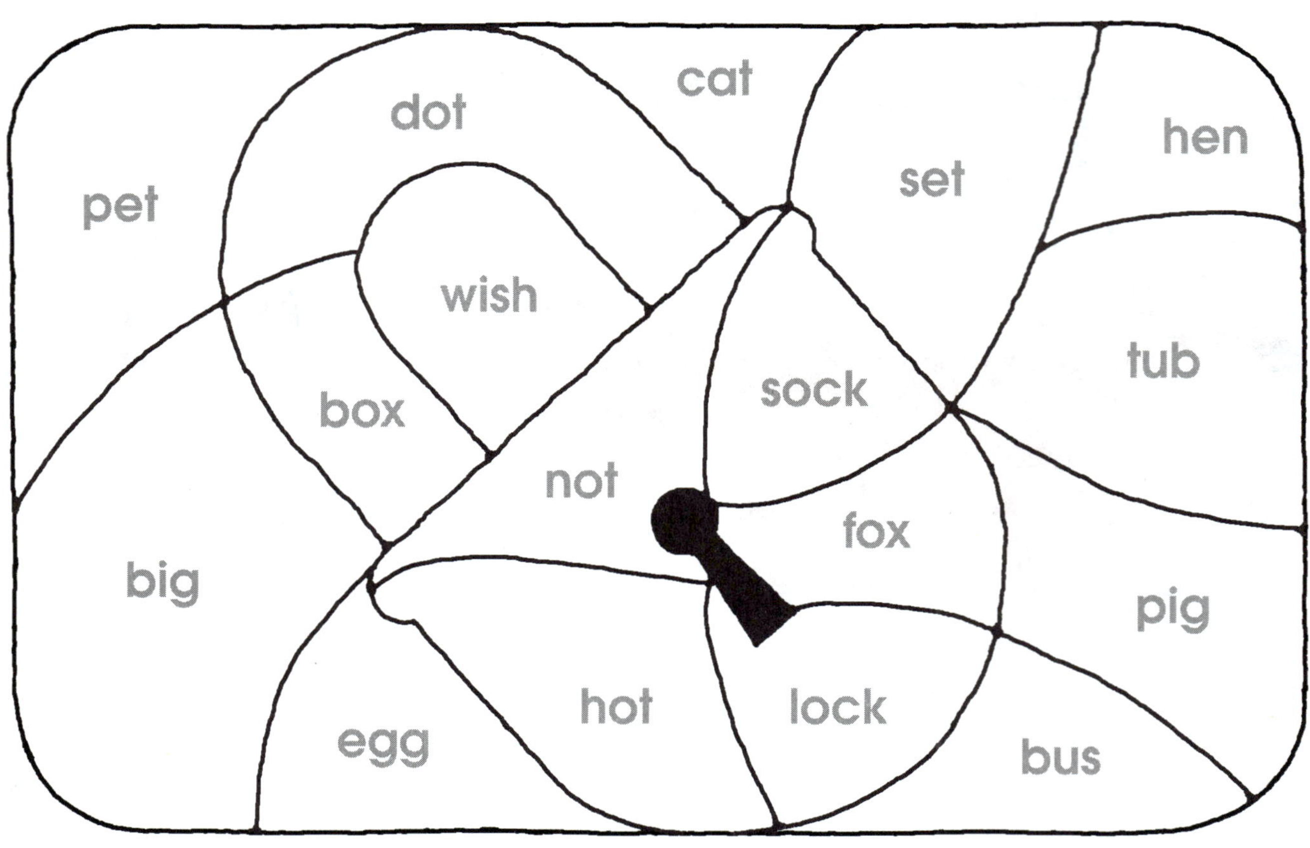

2. This is a picture of a ____________.

3. Write the **short o** words that **end** with **t**.

4. Write the **short o** words that **end** with **x**.

fox clock socks box block pot

Write the **short o** answers to the riddles.

1. You put me on your feet.
   What am I?

2. I hold toys for you.
   What am I?

3. Mom uses me to cook.
   What am I?

4. I'm an animal.
   What am I?

Help! The words got all mixed up.
Write the **short o** words for the pictures.

5. oclkc

6. lcobk

WORDS WITH SHORT o

hop box top not fox got doll mom

1. Write the **short o** words that **rhyme** with **lot**.

2. Write the **short o** words that **rhyme** with **mop**.

3. Write the **short o** words that **end** with **x**.

Write the **short o** words to finish the sentences.

4. Lisa got a ____________ for her birthday.

5. My ____________ is running late today.

1. Color the **short o** words **orange**.

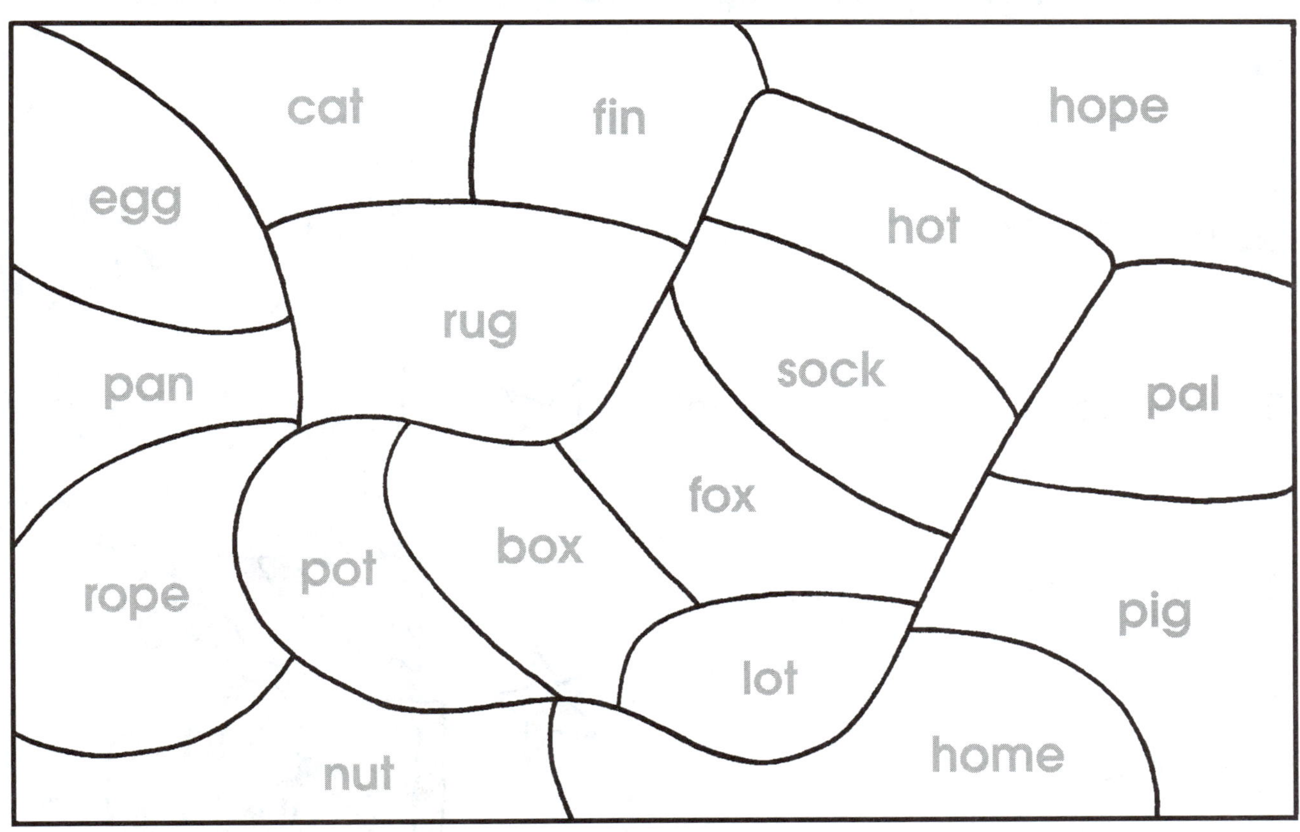

2. Write the **short o** words.

Write the **short o** words to finish the sentences.

fox box pop top mom hot job hop

1. The dog looks like a ________.
2. The soup is too ________ to eat.
3. How far can you ________?
4. We had hot dogs and ________.
5. His ________ said he can go.
6. It is my ________ to set the table.
7. What is in the ________?
8. The book is on the ________ shelf.

WORDS WITH SHORT o

Follow the path of **short o** words.

WORDS WITH SHORT o

Write the **short o** words for the pictures.

doll sock clock mop top box fox block

1. ______

2. ______

3. ______

4. ______

5. ______

6. ______

7. ______

8. ______

WORDS WITH SHORT o

Circle the correct spellings for the **short o** pictures.

1. **box** **bocks**

2. **clock** **clox**

3. **focks** **fox**

4. **socks** **sokcs**

5. **top** **toup**

6. **dowl** **doll**

7. **lok** **lock**

8. **mop** **mopp**

9. **block** **blok**

WORDS WITH SHORT o

Write **o** in the blanks to spell the **short o** words.

1.	2.	3.
n___t	t___p	s___ck
p___t	m___p	l___ck
h___t	h___p	r___ck

got	top	job	doll
lot	box	hot	sock

Write the **short o** words to finish the sentences.

4. Put the toys in the ________.

5. I cannot find my other ________.

6. Be careful, the soup is ________.

7. Zack's father has a new ________.

8. There is snow on ________ of the mountain.

9. Mother made a new dress for my ________.

10. My sister ________ a bike for her birthday.

11. There are a ________ of leaves to rake.

WORDS WITH SHORT i & o

Circle **i** for the words that have the **short i** sound.
Circle **o** for the words that have the **short o** sound.

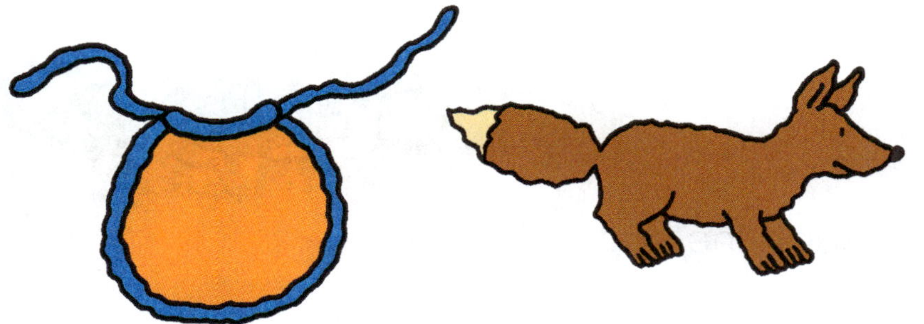

1. **i** **o**
2. **i** **o**
3. **i** **o**

4. **i** **o**
5. **i** **o**
6. **i** **o**

7. **i** **o**
8. **i** **o**
9. **i** **o**

These words have the **short u** sound in umbrella.

sun rug hug
up run

Write the **short u** words that mean the **opposite** of:

1.  down  ______

2.  moon  ______

3.  walk  ______

Write the **short u** words that **begin** with the same letters as the pictures.

4. ______

5. ______

Write the **short u** words for the pictures.

sun bus gum rug duck cup

1.

2.

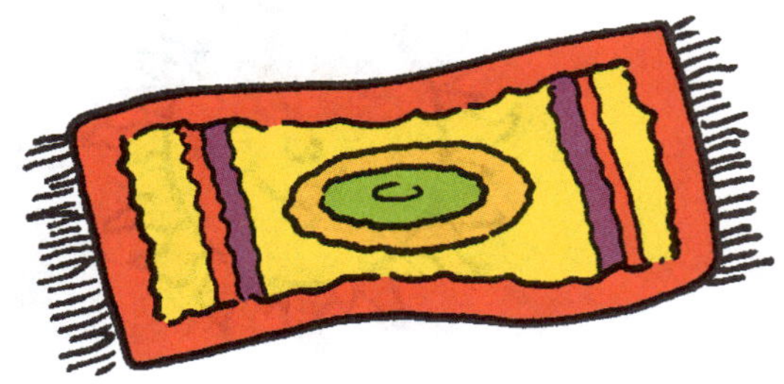

3.

4.

5.

6.

Write the **short u** words for the pictures.

up sun rug run hug bus

1.

2.

3.

4.

5.

6.

nut	up	gum	much
bus	tub	duck	fun

Write the **short u** words that **rhyme** with:

1. **run** ____________
2. **such** ____________
3. **rub** ____________
4. **but** ____________
5. **luck** ____________
6. **cup** ____________
7. **us** ____________
8. **hum** ____________
9. Circle the **short u** words in the word search.

W	H	U	S	D	U	C	K
F	U	N	U	N	X	U	P
L	Z	T	C	U	V	P	V
U	M	U	H	T	R	B	G
C	U	B	B	T	U	U	U
K	C	H	U	M	N	S	M
Z	H	M	T	R	U	B	T

WORDS WITH SHORT u

bug run sun bus gum rug

1. Write the **short u** words that **rhyme** with **fun**.

2. Write the **short u** words that **rhyme** with **hug**.

3. Write the **short u** word that **ends** with **s**.

4. Write the **short u** word that **ends** with **m**.

5. Draw pictures of **short u** words.

bug fun hug duck sun truck

1. Write the **short u** words that **end** with **ug**.

2. Write the **short u** words that **end** with **ck**.

3. Write the **short u** words that **rhyme** with **run**.

4. Help the duck get to the bugs.
   Follow the path of **short u** pictures.

Read the **short u** words in the umbrella.
Write two pairs of words that have the same ending.

gum pup
cup bug hug
fun mud sun

1. ________________ 2. ________________

________________ ________________

Write the beginning letter of each picture to spell **short u** words. The first one is done for you.

3.  +  +  

4. 

+  +  ________________

5.  + 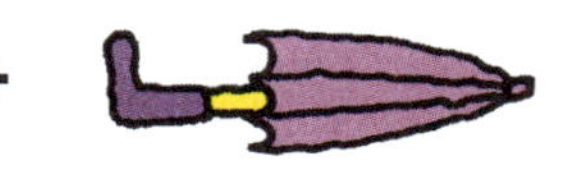 +  ________________

6.   +  + 

____

7.  +  + 

____

8.  + +  ________________

9. 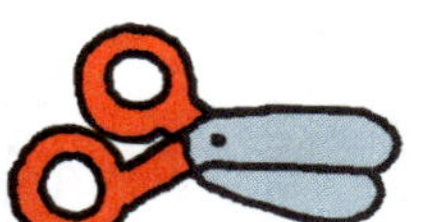 + +  ________________

10.  +  +  ________________

WORDS WITH SHORT u

1. Color the **short u** words **yellow**.

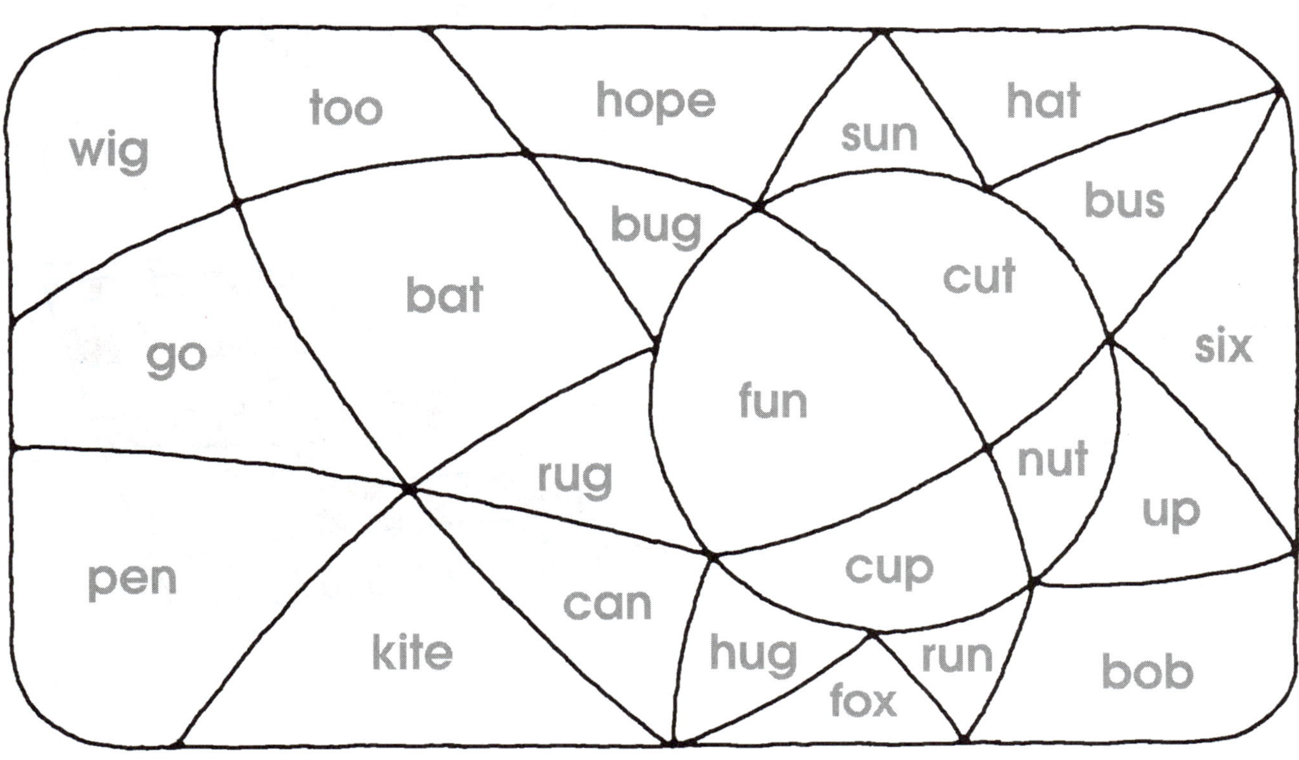

2. This is a picture of a ____________.

3. Add **ug** to make **short u** words.

4. Add **ut** to make **short u** words.

WORDS WITH SHORT u

Write the **short u** words to finish the sentences.

rug mud fun sun cup bus bug run

1. I ride the ____________ to school.

2. We put the ____________ on the floor.

3. It is hot in the ____________.

4. The party was ____________.

5. Did you get ____________ on your shoes?

6. I had to ____________ all the way home.

7. Mom has a new coffee ____________.

8. I do not like that ____________!

Write the **short u** words to finish the sentences.

butter hum gum bun muffin cup lunch nuts

1. I like _______________ on my toast.

2. Put the hot dog in the _______________.

3. What do you have in your _______________?

4. I broke Mom's coffee _______________.

5. Have a blueberry _______________.

6. Squirrels like to eat _______________.

7. Do not chew _______________ in school.

8. Can you _______________ the tune for me?

Circle the **short vowel** words in the word search.

Short a
apple
cat
ant
bat

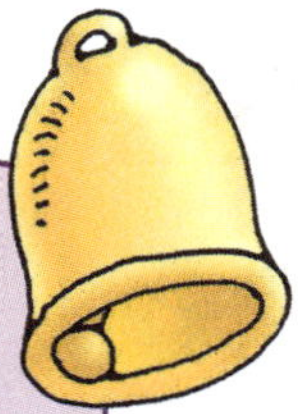

Short e
hen
bell
pet
bed

Short i
pig
fish
big
sit

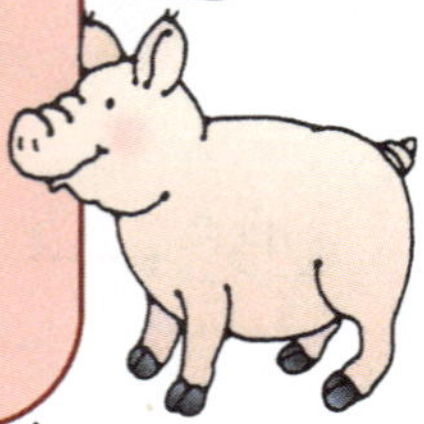

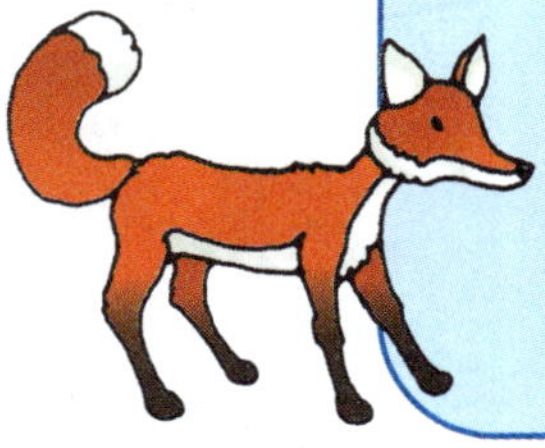

Short o
fox
dog
doll
sock

Short u
bug
cup
sun
duck

I	D	C	A	T	P	Q	Z	S	R
F	O	X	P	B	I	G	C	U	P
B	G	M	P	F	I	S	H	N	W
U	B	D	L	C	E	W	B	Q	I
G	X	Z	E	W	H	P	E	T	O
W	B	A	T	X	S	Z	L	D	P
H	E	N	W	D	O	L	L	U	I
C	D	S	I	T	C	V	W	C	G
A	N	T	Z	Q	K	X	Y	K	W

Finish the words by filling in the missing **short vowels**.
Each word has the same **short vowel** sound as the picture.
Write the words under the correct **vowels** on the word list.

Short a

6. ____________

____

Short e

7. ____________

____

Short i

8. ____________

____

Short o

9. ____________

____

Short u

10. ____________

____

REVIEW: SHORT VOWELS

Write the **short vowels** you hear in the middle of:

1.

2.

3.

4.

5.

6.

7.

8.

9.

10.

REVIEW: SHORT VOWELS

Finish the words by filling in the missing **short vowels**.
Write the words under the correct categories on the word list.

Short a	Short e	Short i	Short o	Short u
1.	2.	3.	4.	5.
h___t	b___lt	p___g	d___ll	d___ck
p___nts	sl___d	f___sh	s___cks	dr___m
b___t			f___x	

6. **Things to wear**	7. **Things to play with**	8. **Animals**
____________	____________	____________
____________	____________	____________
____________	____________	____________
____________	____________	____________

Finish the words by filling in the missing **short vowels**.

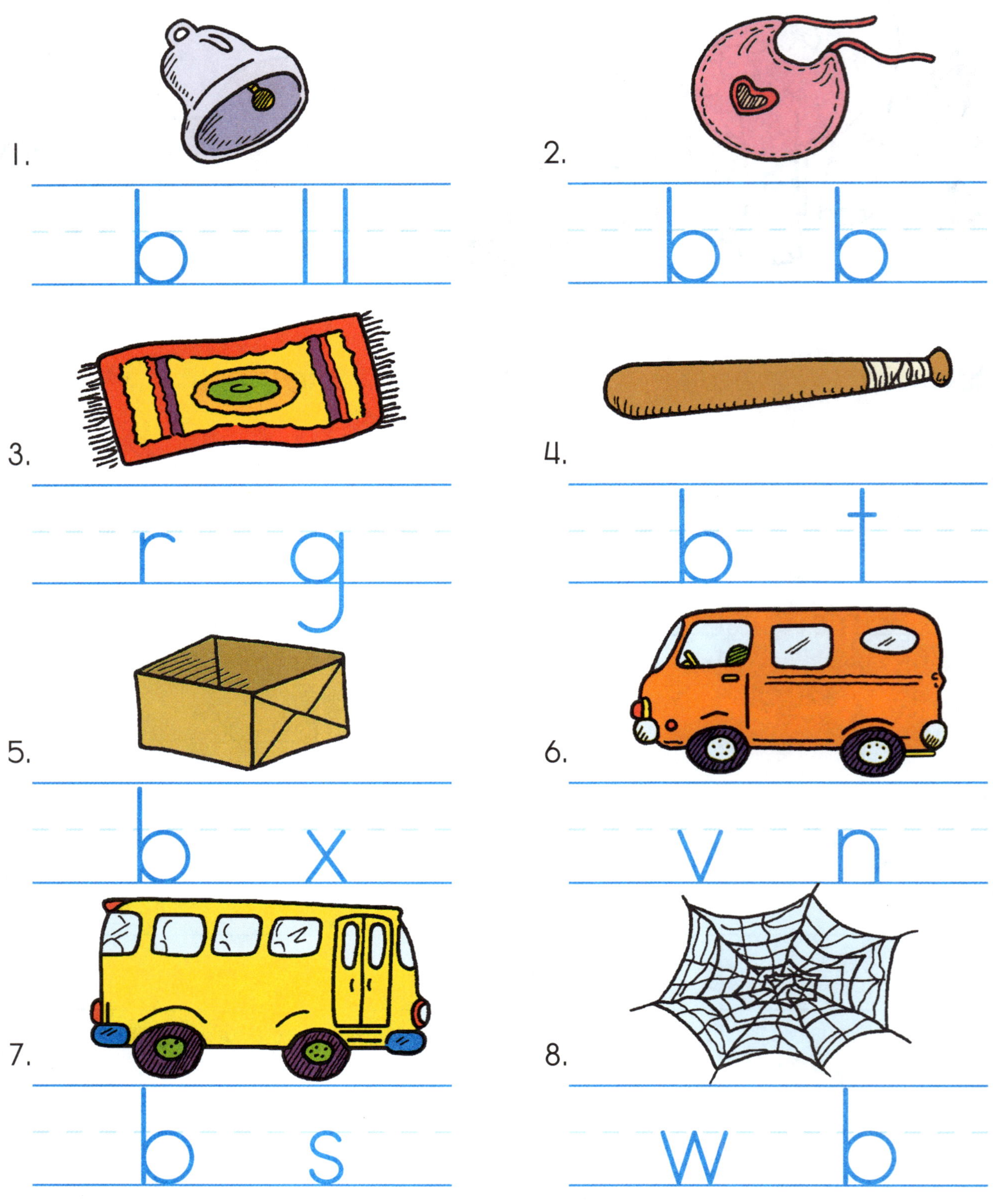

Write the words that have the same **short vowel sounds** as the pictures.

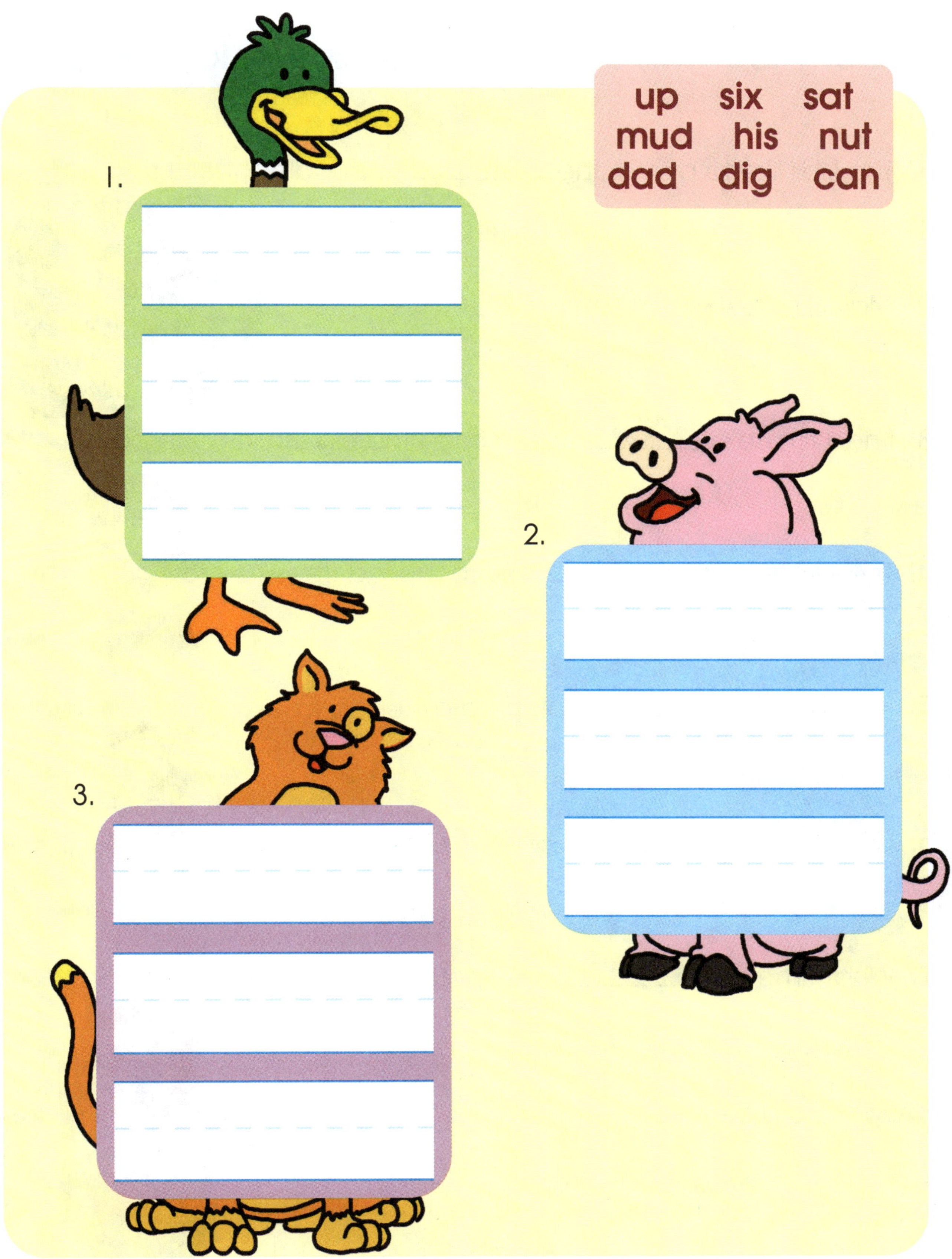

REVIEW: SHORT VOWELS

Write the **short vowel** words to finish the sentences.

hot job his dig net man mud pencil

1. The kids like to play in the ____________ puddles after it rains.

2. May I borrow your ____________ ?

3. I had to use a ____________ to bring the big fish into the boat.

4. The pirate likes to ____________ for buried treasure.

5. It is my ____________ to cut the grass each week.

6. On a ____________ day, we like to go swimming.

7. What time does ____________ mother want him to come home?

8. Joey paid the ____________ for his ticket.

Write the **short vowel** words for the pictures.

bat box fish dish hen ten rug hat

1.

2.

3.

4.

5.

6.

7.

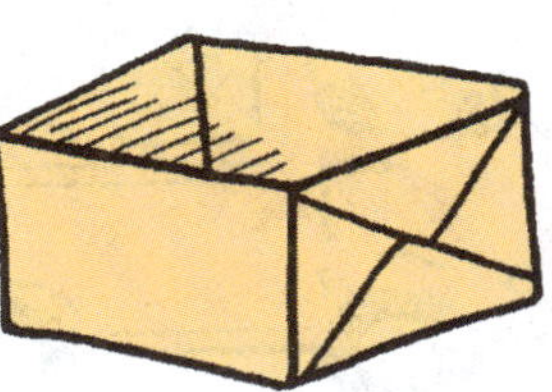

8.

Write the **short vowel** words for the pictures.

cat net drum bib van fox sock bed

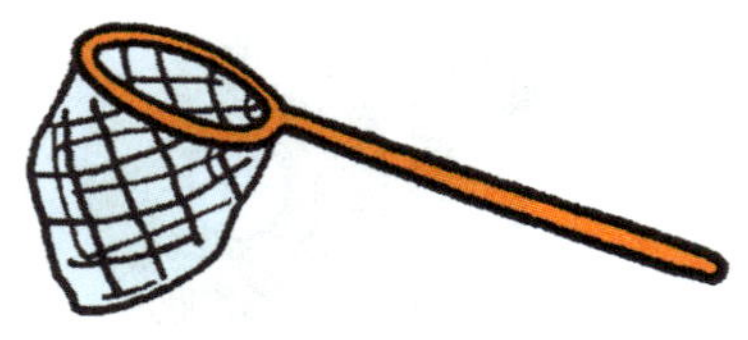

1.

2.

3.

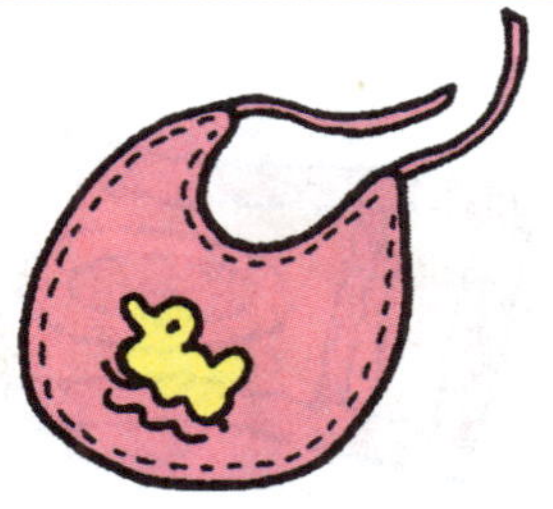

4.

5.

6.

7.

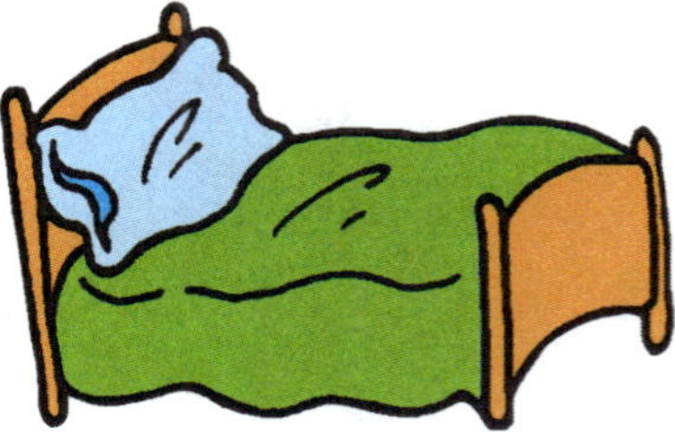

8.

Write the **short vowel** words for the pictures.

duck pig nest desk lock can ten cup

1. 

2. 

3. 

4. 

5. 

6. 

7. 

8. 

Read the clues.
Write the **short vowel** answers in the puzzle.

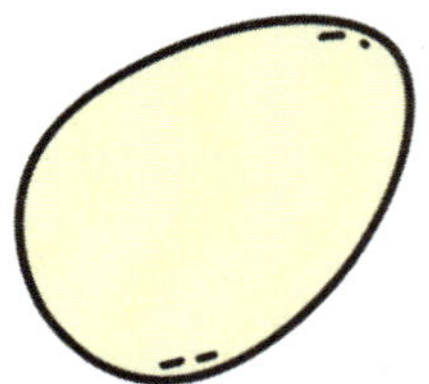

sun
egg
socks
pig
hat
ten

Across

2. You wear _____ on your feet.
3. _____ is the number after 9.
5. A _____ says "oink".

Down

1. You wear a _____ on your head.
2. Plants need _____ and water to grow.
4. A bird hatches from an _____.

WORDS WITH LONG a

These words have the **long a** sound in .

rake **game** **tape** **vase** **cake** **gate**

Write the **long a** words to answer the riddles.

1. You can put flowers in me.
   What am I?

2. You like to eat me.
   What am I?

3. I fix a torn page.
   What am I?

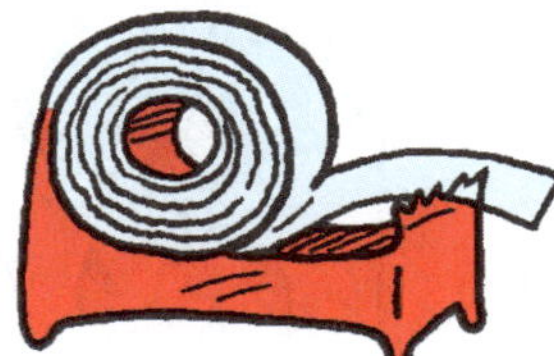

4. You use me to pile leaves.
   What am I?

5. Write the **long a** words that **begin** with **g**.

WORDS WITH LONG a

Silly Snail is on the trail to get her pail.
What did she see on the way?
Write the **long a** words by the pictures.

jay mail train tray rain
paint pail hay chain snail

WORDS WITH LONG a

Write the **long a** words for the pictures.

paint rain made say wait cake hay train

1. 

2. 

3.

4. 

5. 

6. 

7. 

8. 

WORDS WITH LONG a

Write the **long a** words for the pictures.

jay rake crayon game vase gate

1.

2.

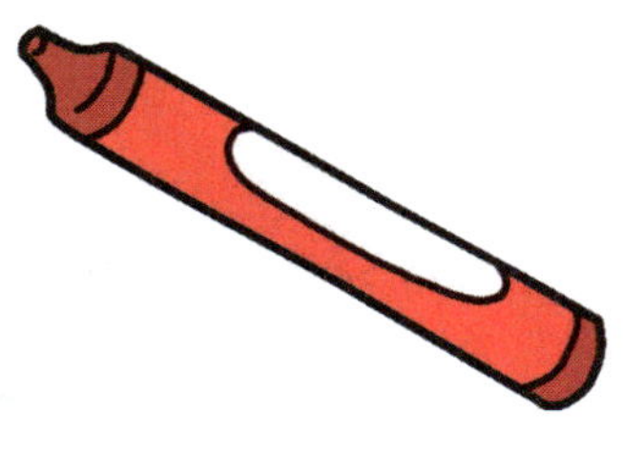

3.

4.

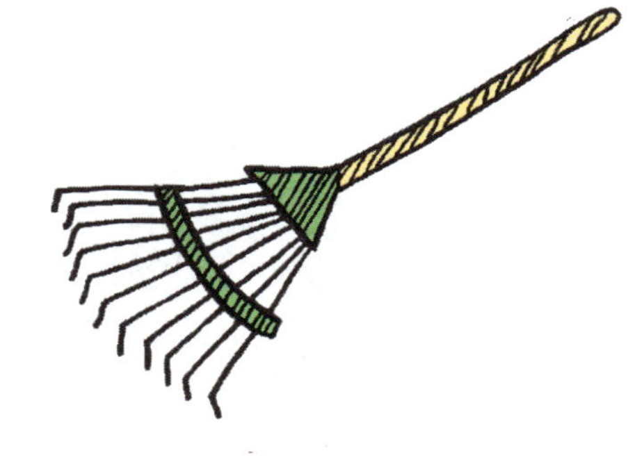

5.

6.

Write the **long a** words for the pictures.

mail nail rain train quail pail paint snail

1.

2.

3.

4.

5.

6.

7.

8.

WORDS WITH LONG a

Write the **long a** words for the pictures.

tray spray jay hay crayon play

1. 

2. 

3.

4. 

5. Find the **long a** words in the word search.

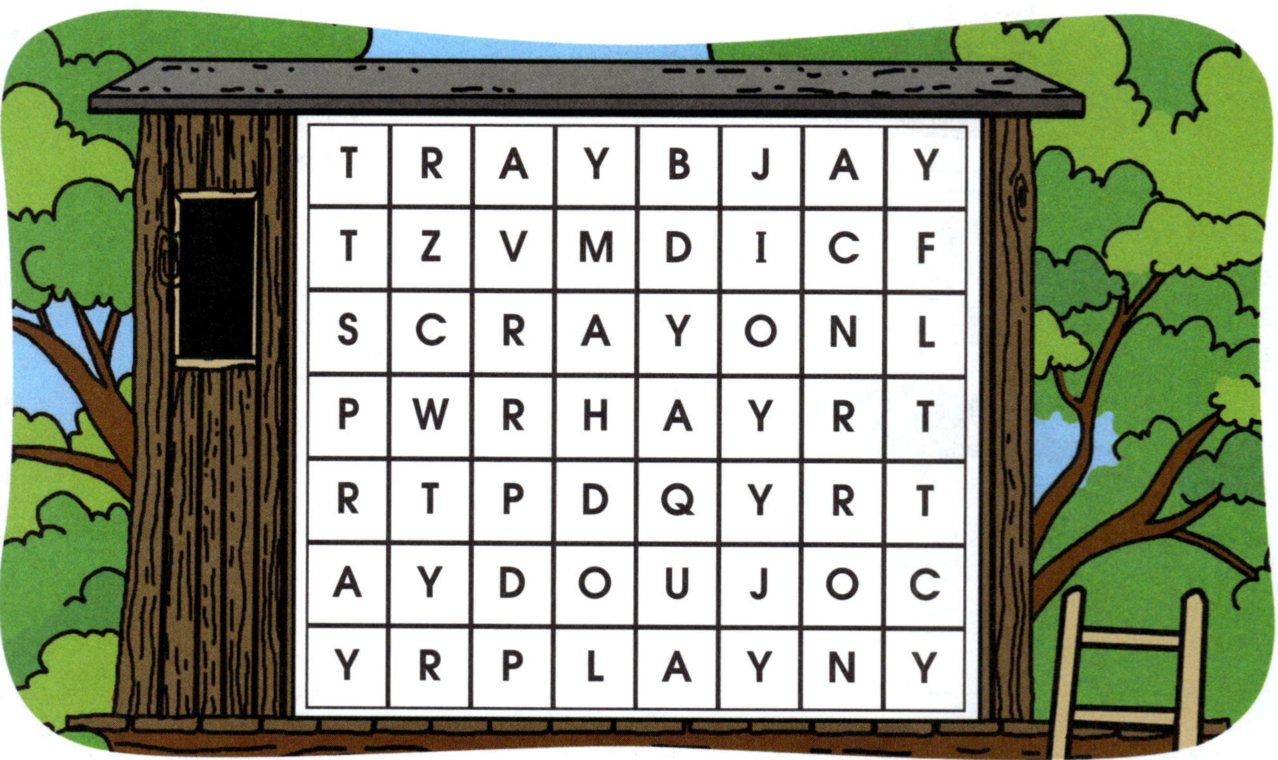

T	R	A	Y	B	J	A	Y
T	Z	V	M	D	I	C	F
S	C	R	A	Y	O	N	L
P	W	R	H	A	Y	R	T
R	T	P	D	Q	Y	R	T
A	Y	D	O	U	J	O	C
Y	R	P	L	A	Y	N	Y

WORDS WITH LONG a

Write the **long a** words to finish the sentences.

eight wait tame play say ate name late

1. What is your ____________?

2. Brad has a ____________ rabbit.

3. You do not have to ____________ for me.

4. I have a role in the school ____________.

5. Don't be ____________ for dinner.

6. Who ____________ the last piece of pie?

7. What did your mother ____________?

8. Bedtime is at ____________ o'clock.

WORDS WITH LONG a

The Great Longo is a magician. He makes **long vowel** words!
Write the **long a** words for the pictures.
Then write the **long a** words on Longo's magic chain.

sail nail snail pail rain train

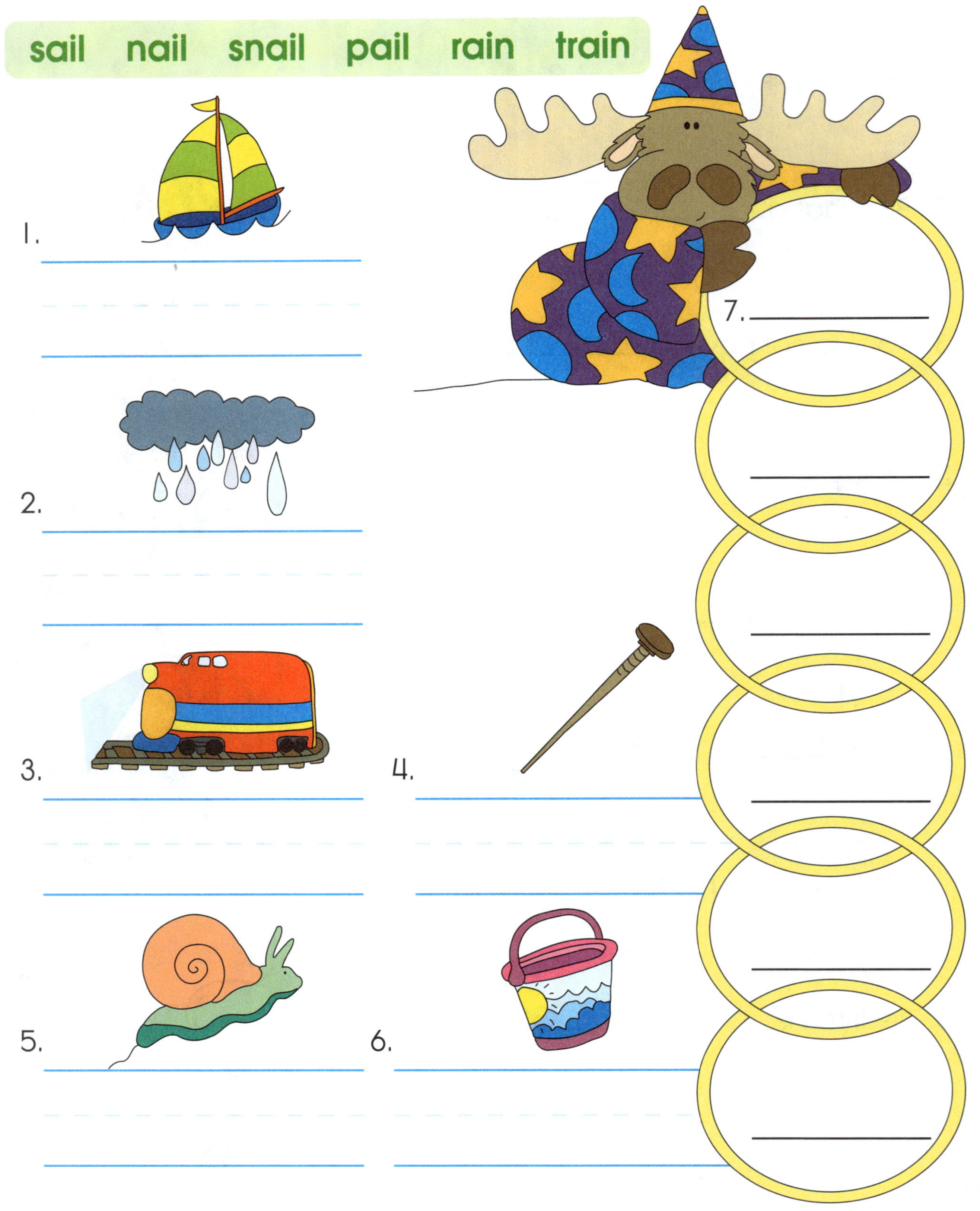

WORDS WITH LONG a

Make a **long a** playhouse! Make it with **ay** bricks!
Write the **long a** words for the pictures.
Then write the **long a** words on the bricks of the playhouse.

tray crayon jay play spray hay

1. ______________

2. ______________

3. ______________

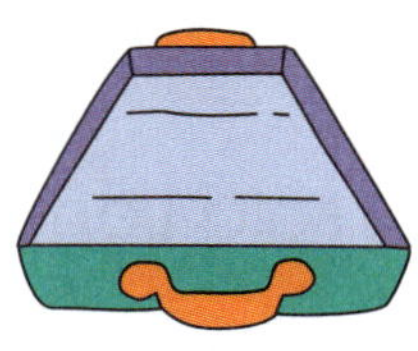

4. ______________

5. ______________

6. ______________

7. ______________ ______________ ______________ ______________ ______________ ______________

The Great Longo had a **long a** party.
He called it the sleigh ride party.
Use the **eigh** words to finish the sentences.
Then read the story to find out
what happened.

eight **eighty-eight**
Neigh **weigh**
sleigh **Eight**

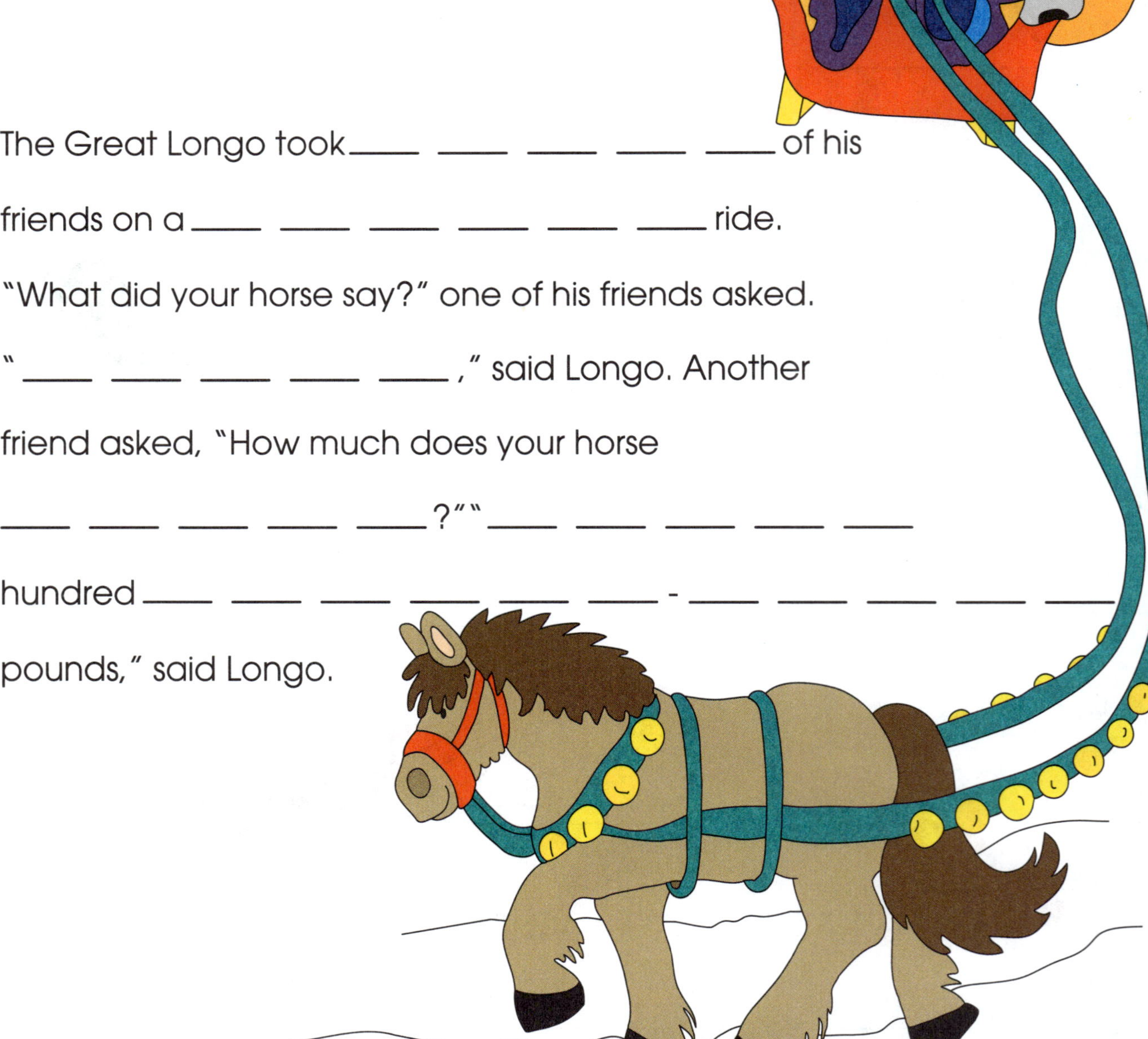

The Great Longo took ____ ____ ____ ____ ____ of his friends on a ____ ____ ____ ____ ____ ____ ride.

"What did your horse say?" one of his friends asked.

" ____ ____ ____ ____ ____ ," said Longo. Another friend asked, "How much does your horse ____ ____ ____ ____ ____?" " ____ ____ ____ ____ ____ hundred ____ ____ ____ ____ ____ ____ - ____ ____ ____ ____ ____ pounds," said Longo.

The Great Longo has a **silent e** wand!
The **silent e** wand changes words.
Many words with **long vowel sounds** are spelled with a **vowel**, a **consonant**, and then **e**.

made

mane cane cape made

Add **e** to the bold words to make **long a** words.

1. The **man** was on a horse with a nice ___ ___ ___ ___.

2. He hit the **can** with his ___ ___ ___ ___.

3. Are you **mad** that I ___ ___ ___ ___ you practice?

4. The magician's **cap** matched his ___ ___ ___ ___.

WORDS WITH LONG a

The Great Longo is still making **long a** words with the **silent e** wand.

fade same
pale plane made

Add **e** to the bold words to make **long a** words.

1. I ____ ____ ____ ____ my mother **mad**.
2. My **pal** looked sick and ____ ____ ____ ____.
3. **Sam** is on the ____ ____ ____ ____ team as Joe.
4. I **plan** to fly on a ____ ____ ____ ____ ____.
5. It is a **fad** to ____ ____ ____ ____ jeans.

Write the **long a** words to finish the story.

A Snail on a Trail

Follow the ____________.

He is on the ____________.

The ____________ won't slow him down.

No, it won't keep him ____________.

He doesn't want to be ____________.

He wants to ____________ with his friends.

Maybe he will need to take the ____________.

rain
trail
snail
away
train
play
late

WORDS WITH LONG a

Write the **long a** words for the pictures.
Then draw lines to match the words that **rhyme**.

cake play plane snail train snake day pail

1. 

2. 

3. 

4. 

5. 

6. 

7. 

8. 

The Great Longo is on the **long a** train.
Fill the train cars with **long a** words.
Write only the **long a** words on the cars of the train.

ran day sad bat
hat ask bake mad
stay car made pail

These words have the **long e** sound in .

he me
see three
tree she

1. Write the 2-letter **long e** words that **rhyme** with **bee**.

2. Write the 3-letter **long e** words that **rhyme** with **bee**.

Write the **long e** words for the pictures.

3.

4.

WORDS WITH LONG e

meet seal she feet be leaf

1. Write the **long e** words that are spelled with **ee**.

2. Write the **long e** words that **end** with **e**.

Write the **long e** words for the pictures.

3.

4.

5. Add **ea** to finish the **long e** words.

t m m t

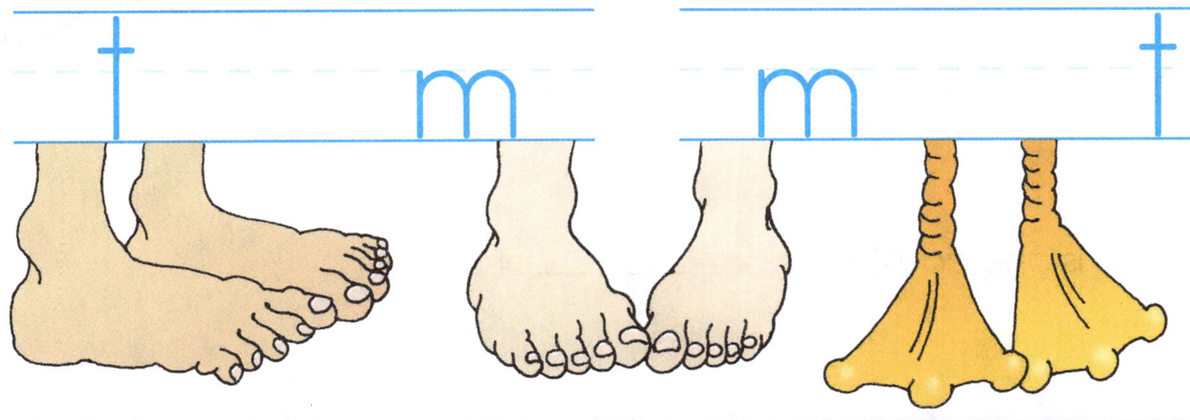

WORDS WITH LONG e

Write the **long e** words to finish the sentences.

feel peas sheep each read teeth keep team

1. Little Bo Peep lost her ____________ .

2. May I ____________ the pen you let me use?

3. I think it is easier to eat ____________ with a spoon!

4. Did you brush your ____________ this morning?

5. I asked my mother to ____________ a story to me.

6. I think fish ____________ slimy.

7. Our ____________ won first place in the race.

8. There is one cookie for ____________ of us.

Write the **long e** words to finish the story.
Then underline the other **long e** words in the story.

seeds sweet honey creek field beach

The Big Sleep

The bee dreamed of ____________.

The turkey dreamed of ____________.

The geese dreamed of a ____________.

The sheep dreamed of a ____________.

The baby dreamed of something ____________.

And I dreamed of the ____________.

Read the clues.
Write the **long e** answers in the puzzle.

see	bean	key
clean	leave	seed
money	dream	tree

Across

2. produces a plant
5. go away
7. used to buy things
8. a kind of vegetable

Down

1. a large plant
2. look at
3. happens when asleep
4. the opposite of dirty
6. opens a lock

WORDS WITH LONG e

1. Color the **long e** words **green**.

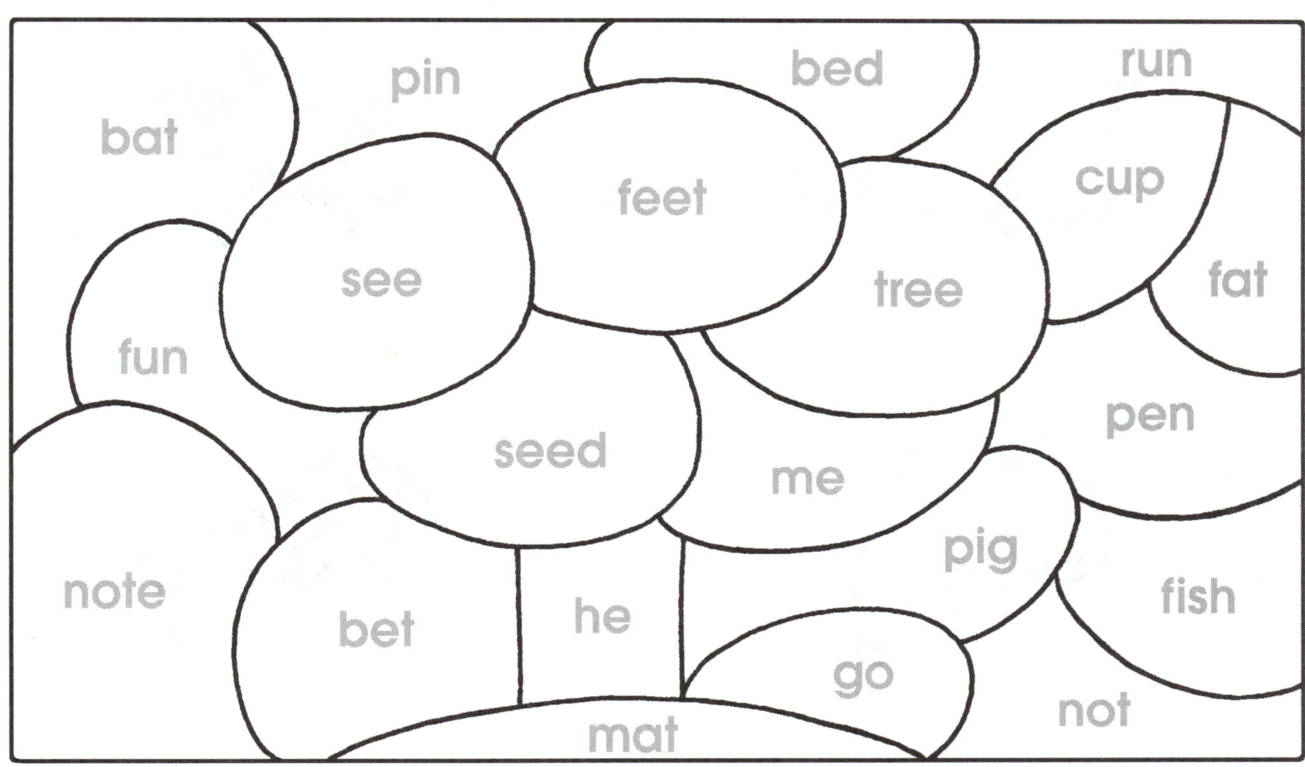

2. Write the **long e** words.

Write the **long e** words for the pictures.

leaf seal meat beads eagle peas peach jeans

1.

2.

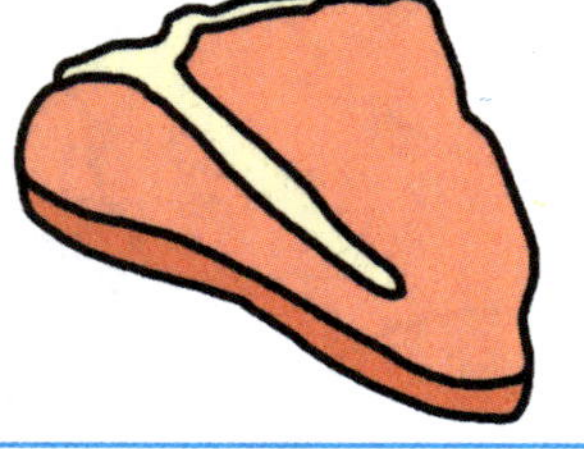

3.

4.

5.

6.

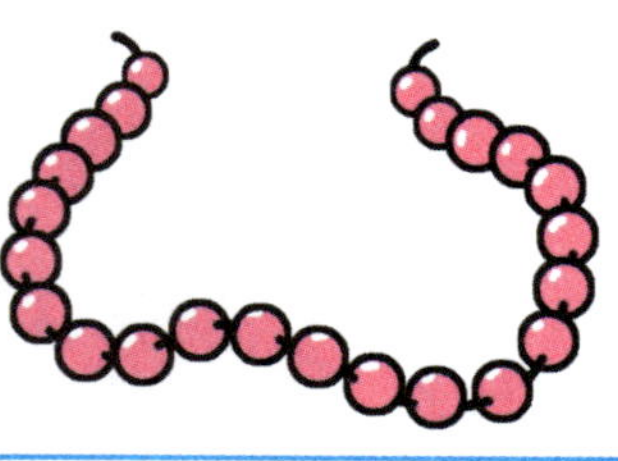

7.

8.

WORDS WITH LONG e

Write the **long e** words for the pictures.

three bee he key tree monkey sheep she

1.

2.

3.

4.

5.

6.

7.

8.

WORDS WITH LONG e

This bee is looking for **long e** words.
Write the **long e** words for the pictures.

sheep	teeth	three
teepee	wheel	tree

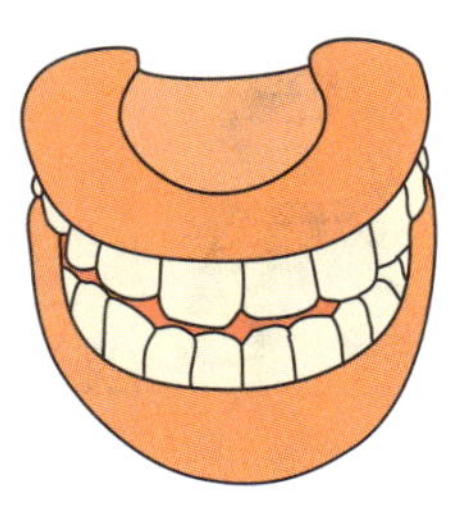

1. ______________

2. ______________

3. ______________

4. ______________

5. ______________

6. ______________

Write the **long e** words to answer the riddles.

bee seal me tree he leaf

1. I can swim.

2. I am a large plant.

3. I grow on a tree.

4. I get food from flowers.

5. Write the 2-letter **long e** words.

WORDS WITH LONG e

Write the **long e** words for the pictures.

beads jeans seal beak
peanut eagle leaf meat

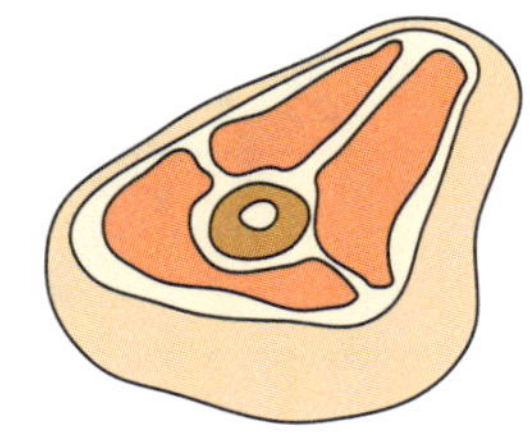

1.

2.

3.

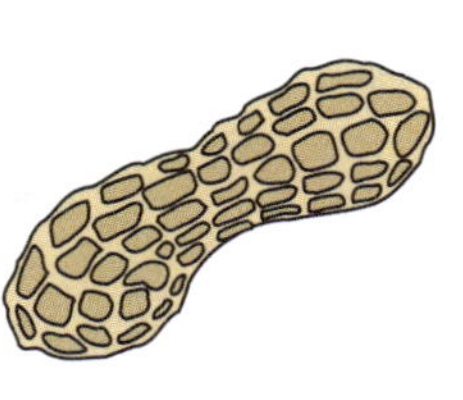

4.

5.

6.

7.

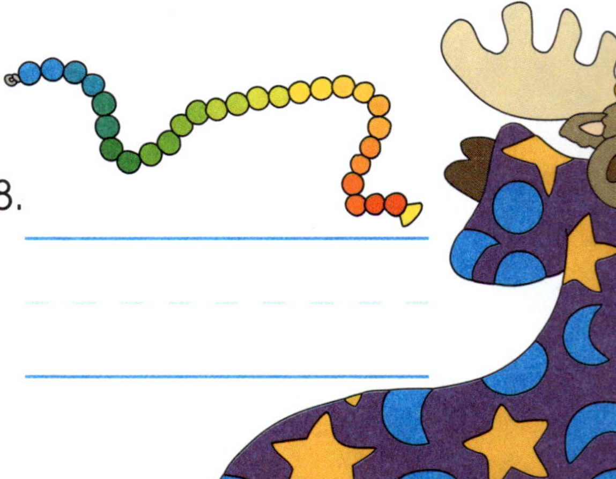

8.

Write **long e** words by adding the missing letters **ey**.
Draw lines from the pictures to the **long e** words.

key
turkey
money
hockey
monkey
donkey

1. k___ ___

2. monk___ ___

3. donk___ ___

4. hock___ ___

5. mon___ ___

6. turk___ ___

Look at all of these **long e** words made with **ey**!

Help the Great Longo catch a thief!
Write the **long e** words for the pictures.

WORDS WITH LONG e

Find the **long e** words in the word search.

cookie	key	peanut	bee	turkey
teepee	tree	wheel	leaf	penny

T	U	R	K	E	Y	T	V	X	Q
R	B	W	H	A	O	R	C	N	P
C	X	Z	W	D	N	E	P	T	E
W	C	O	O	K	I	E	E	X	A
R	S	Q	R	B	T	V	N	W	N
X	K	W	H	E	E	L	N	V	U
C	E	N	B	E	W	E	Y	S	T
P	Y	V	D	X	C	A	F	G	J
T	E	E	P	E	E	F	H	K	L

WORDS WITH LONG i

These words have the **long i** sound in .

kite tie fine bike like ride

Write the **long i** words to answer the riddles.

1. You can fly me.
   What am I?

2. You can ride me.
   What am I?

3. I am something to wear.
   What am I?

Write the **long i** words that fit these shapes.

4.

5.

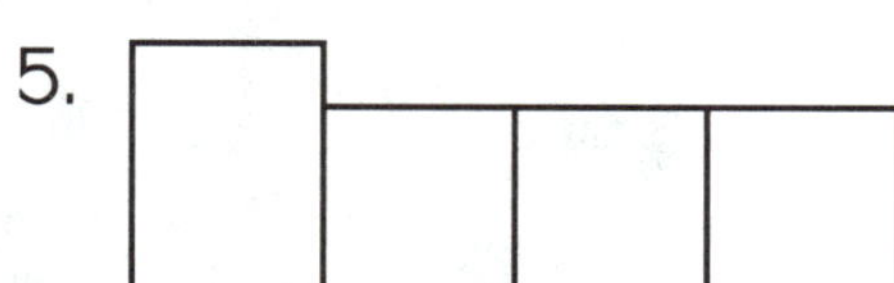

6.

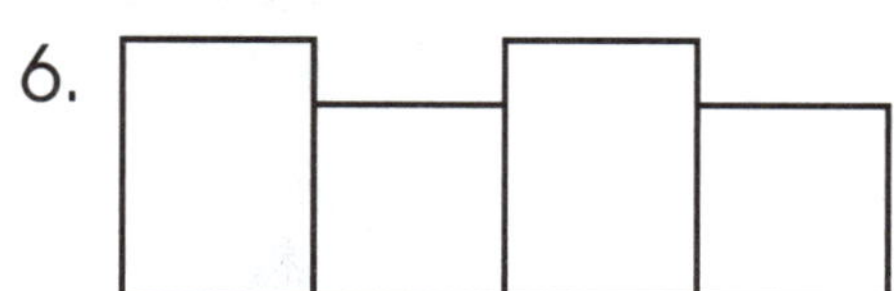

Write the **long i** words to finish the sentences.

kite mile five pie bite time nice dime

1. Our dog had __________ puppies.
2. The __________ flew into a tree.
3. Mother made an apple __________ .
4. Jon walked a __________ to school.
5. My dog won't __________ .
6. Our new teacher is __________ .
7. It is __________ to go now.
8. A __________ is worth ten pennies.

Write the **long i** words for the pictures.

dime kite write time tire bike fire hive

1. ______________________

2. ______________________

3. ______________________

4. ______________________

5. ______________________

6. ______________________

7. ______________________

8. ______________________

WORDS WITH LONG i

kind find try night cry right

1. Write the **long i** words that **end** with **d**.

2. Write the **long i** words that **rhyme** with **kite**.

3. Write the **long i** words that **end** with **y**.

4. Underline the **long i** words in the story.

My friend and I took a hike up a hill.

We flew our kites high in the sky.

My friend and I had a fun time.

1. Color the **long i** words **purple**.

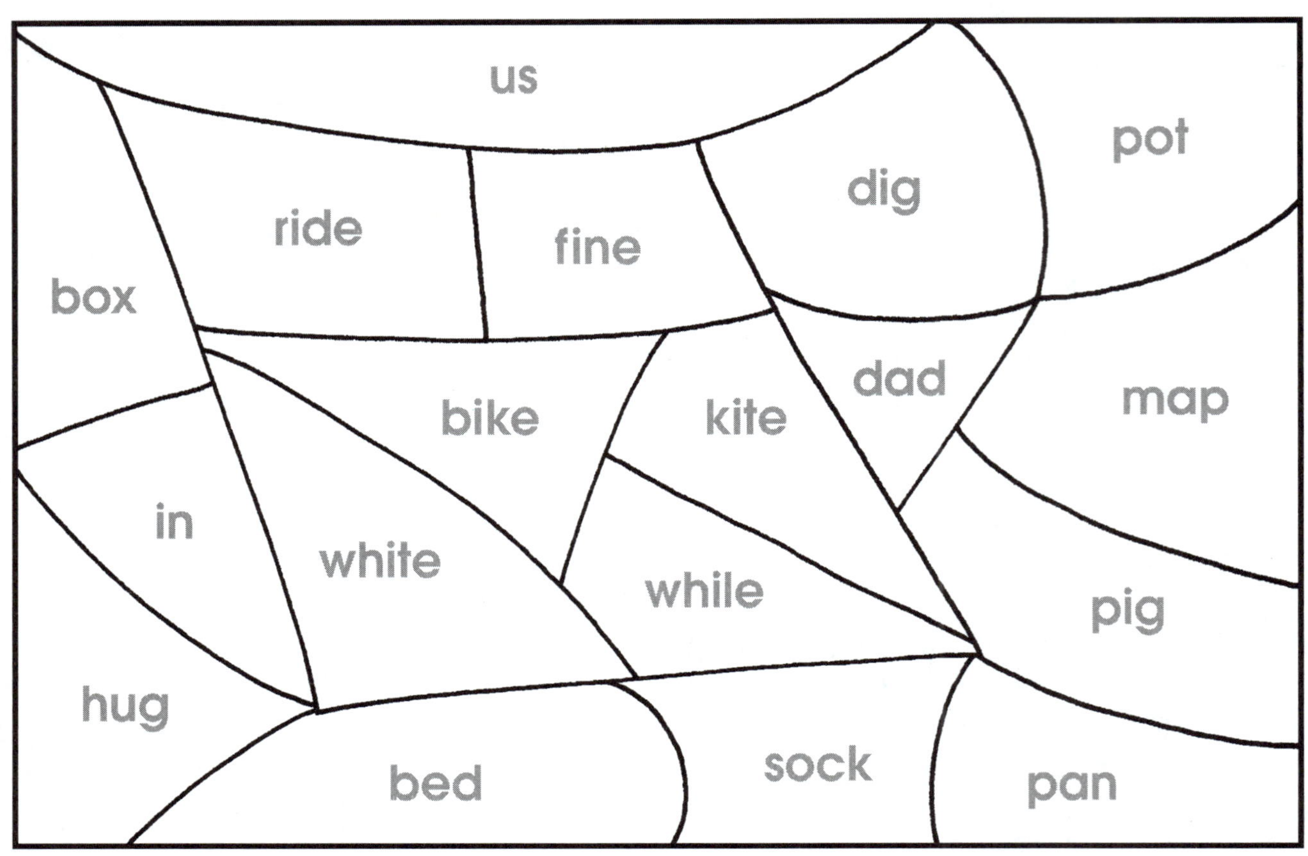

2. Write the **long i** words.

The Great Longo makes **long i** words. He uses the letters **ie** or the letter **y**. The Great Longo is tricky! Fill in the blanks with the paired words that rhyme.

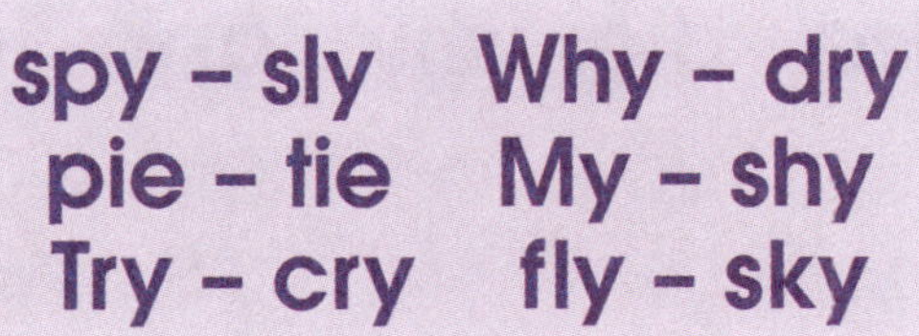

1. Birds ____________ in the ____________.

2. A ____________ must be very ____________.

3. ____________ sister is very ____________.

4. ____________ not let our paintings ____________?

5. Some ____________ fell on my ____________.

6. ____________ not to ____________.

WORDS WITH LONG i

Write the **long i** words to finish the sentences.

hide tire size die shy cry like line

1. Our car has a flat ____________.

2. The boys are the same ____________.

3. I heard the baby ____________ for her mother.

4. Maisy looks ____________ her mom.

5. We waited in ____________ for the bus.

6. A deer is a ____________ animal.

7. A plant will ____________ without water.

8. We like to ____________ Easter eggs.

Find the **long i** words in the word search.

fly	night	mice	cry	vine	tire
nice	kind	nine	right	sky	line

U	F	L	Y	A	N	I	G	H	T
M	N	T	P	Q	I	R	M	P	N
I	L	M	Z	H	N	I	C	E	T
C	M	B	R	W	E	K	S	L	I
E	Q	K	I	N	D	C	T	I	R
X	V	Z	G	W	N	P	Q	N	E
E	O	X	H	B	L	C	S	E	M
M	P	V	T	W	X	Y	K	Q	H
V	I	N	E	Z	C	R	Y	N	I

WORDS WITH LONG i

Write the **long i** words to answer the riddles.

ice five dime pie fire bike

1. I have two wheels. 

2. I am a coin that's worth 10¢. 

3. I am very hot. 

4. I am the number after 4. 

Write the **long i** words for the pictures.

5. 

6. 

WORDS WITH LONG i

Mighty Lion is chasing the Great Longo.
Write the **long i** words for the pictures.

WORDS WITH LONG i

The Great Longo is making riddles.
The answers are **long i** words that end in **ild** or **ind**.
Write the **long i** words to answer the riddles.

blind	mind
wild	find
kind	child

1. If you help people, you are ____________ .

2. A baby is a ____________ .

3. I think with my ____________.

4. If you can't see, you are ____________ .

5. If you lose a toy, you try to ____________ it.

6. A horse that is not tame is ____________ .

WORDS WITH LONG i

Write the **long i** words that have the same endings.

cry nine find fly night vine mind right

1. try

2. kind

3. might

4. fine

5. Add **ight** to make **long i** words.

l

t

WORDS WITH LONG i

Write the **long i** words for the pictures.

island lime tiger ice fire vine mice five

1. 

2. 

3. 

4. 

5. 

6. 

7. 

8. 

WORDS WITH LONG i

Find the **long i** words in the word search.

bike sight write lie fire sky ice wife pie might

S	B	G	W	C	P	A	Q	T	W
I	X	V	R	M	I	W	F	G	I
G	H	B	I	K	E	Z	P	Z	F
H	K	A	T	V	M	R	T	S	E
T	L	I	E	P	N	Q	Y	K	M
V	X	C	F	Z	Y	A	N	P	W
A	W	M	I	G	H	T	X	G	Y
W	S	K	Y	F	R	F	I	R	E
B	G	H	I	C	E	J	L	K	P

WORDS WITH LONG i

Write the **long i** words to finish the sentences.

pie five hive tie drive spider nice

1. Please be ____________ to everyone.
2. Would you like the last piece of ____________?
3. Some bees made a ____________ in our tree.
4. Kaden will be ____________ on his next birthday.
5. My older brother can ____________ the tractor.
6. I bought my dad a ____________ .
7. I see a ____________ in the web.

WORDS WITH LONG o

These words have the **long o** sound in .

show hold boat told grow goat note home

Write the **long o** words to finish the sentences.

1. What did the __________ say?

Mom,
I went to Brenda's
to play. I will be
home at 4:30.
Love,
Sue

2. The __________ sailed across the lake.

3. Who __________ you the joke?

4. How high will the tree __________?

5. We saw a good __________ on TV last night.

6. The __________ has horns.

7. It is time to go __________.

8. Please __________ my hand.

Write the **long o** words that fit the clues.

go most own sold no old both hold

1. not young ____________
2. opposite of yes ____________
3. yours only ____________
4. keep ____________
5. more than more ____________
6. two ____________
7. opposite of bought ____________
8. opposite of stop ____________

WORDS WITH LONG o

Write the **long o** words to finish the sentences.

show low road grow snow goat slow coat

1. Will it ____________ today?

2. The ____________ is bumpy.

3. My ____________ keeps me warm.

4. It jumped over a ____________ wall.

5. Will you ____________ me how it works?

6. The clock is ____________.

7. Did the ____________ eat the apple?

8. The tree will ____________ very high.

1. Color the **long o** words **blue**.

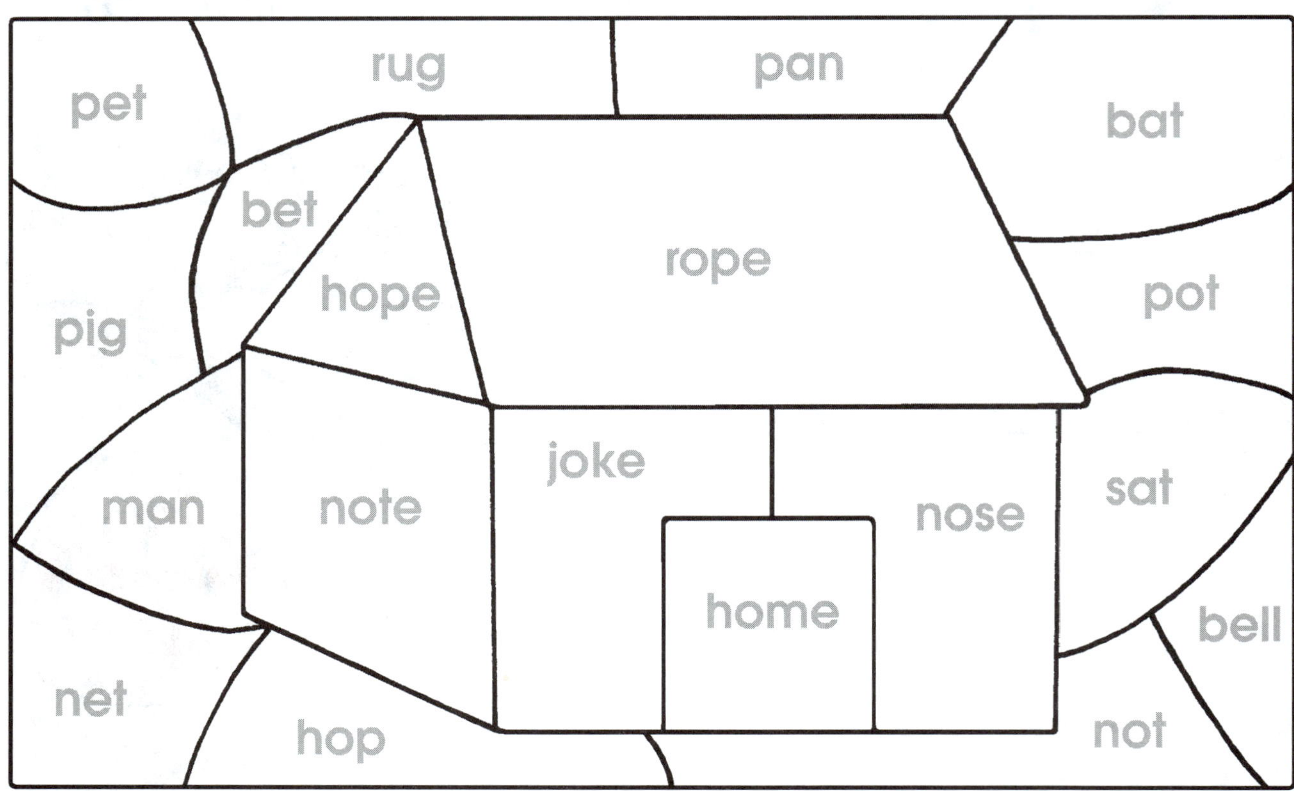

2. Write the **long o** words.

Read the clues.
Write the **long o** answers in the puzzle.

snow goat toast road
show low slow grow

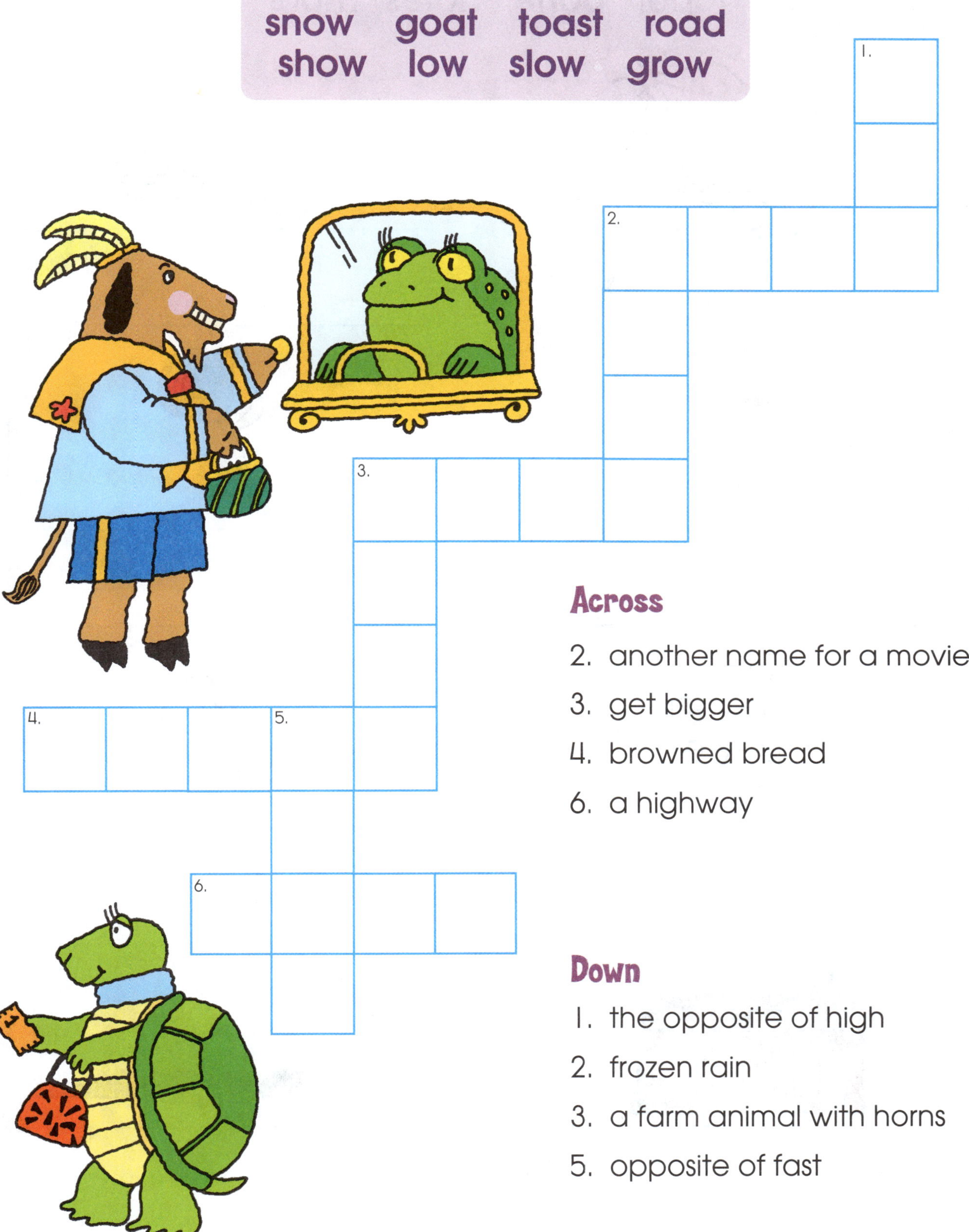

Across

2. another name for a movie
3. get bigger
4. browned bread
6. a highway

Down

1. the opposite of high
2. frozen rain
3. a farm animal with horns
5. opposite of fast

Write the **long o** words for the pictures.

hole rose rope bone notes mole pole home

1. 

2. 

3.

4. 

5. 

6. 

7.

8. 

Write only the **long o** words inside the globe.

globe told rope now row not
goat top got toe lot home

WORDS WITH LONG o

Write the **long o** words that **rhyme** with:

show road hole goat rose no most hold

1. **gold** ____________

2. **ghost** ____________

3. **pole** ____________

4. **nose** ____________

5. **go** ____________

6. **coat** ____________

7. **toad** ____________

8. **slow** ____________

Write the **long o** words for the pictures.

goat toast doe hoe
toad coat toe road boat

1. 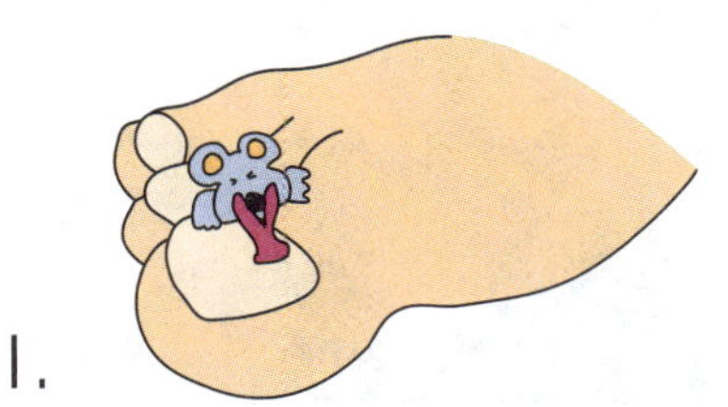

2. 

3. 

4. 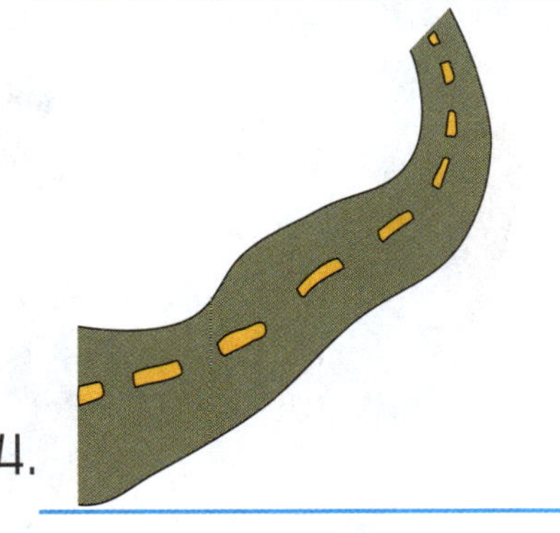

5. 

6. 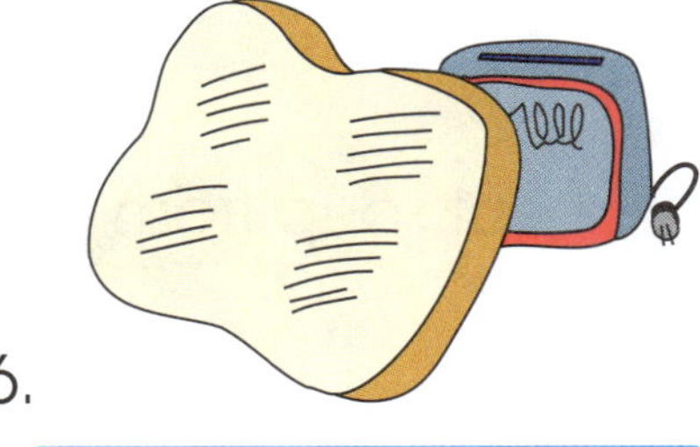

7. 

8. 

9. 

WORDS WITH LONG o

The Great Longo is making **long o** sentences.
He makes the **long o** sound with **o**, **ow**, **old**, or **ost**.
How tricky!
Write the **long o** words to finish the sentences.

old crow
no ghost bowl
go snow Gold

1. Get ready, get set, ____________!

2. I eat soup from a ____________.

3. White ____________ fell from the sky.

4. ____________ is bright and shiny.

5. Did you see a ____________ on Halloween?

6. That black bird is a ____________.

7. If it is not yes, it is ____________.

8. How ____________ are you?

Help the Great Longo find the **long o** words in the word search.

nose rope pole home hole mole bone rose

C M O L E J P G E S
V L N P B D K A R N
X G H O M E Q V O K
T N C L J T K X Z P
R O P E Y Q B R S T
Z S B C N R O S E U
O E J A D K N V W Y
N M V H O L E Z B D
P K T L A C V W Y N

WORDS WITH LONG o

snow cold slow told grow sold

1. Write the **long o** words that are spelled with **ow**.

2. Write the **long o** words that are spelled with **old**.

3. Color the **long o** words that are spelled with **ow black**.
   Color the **long o** words that are spelled with **old** yellow.

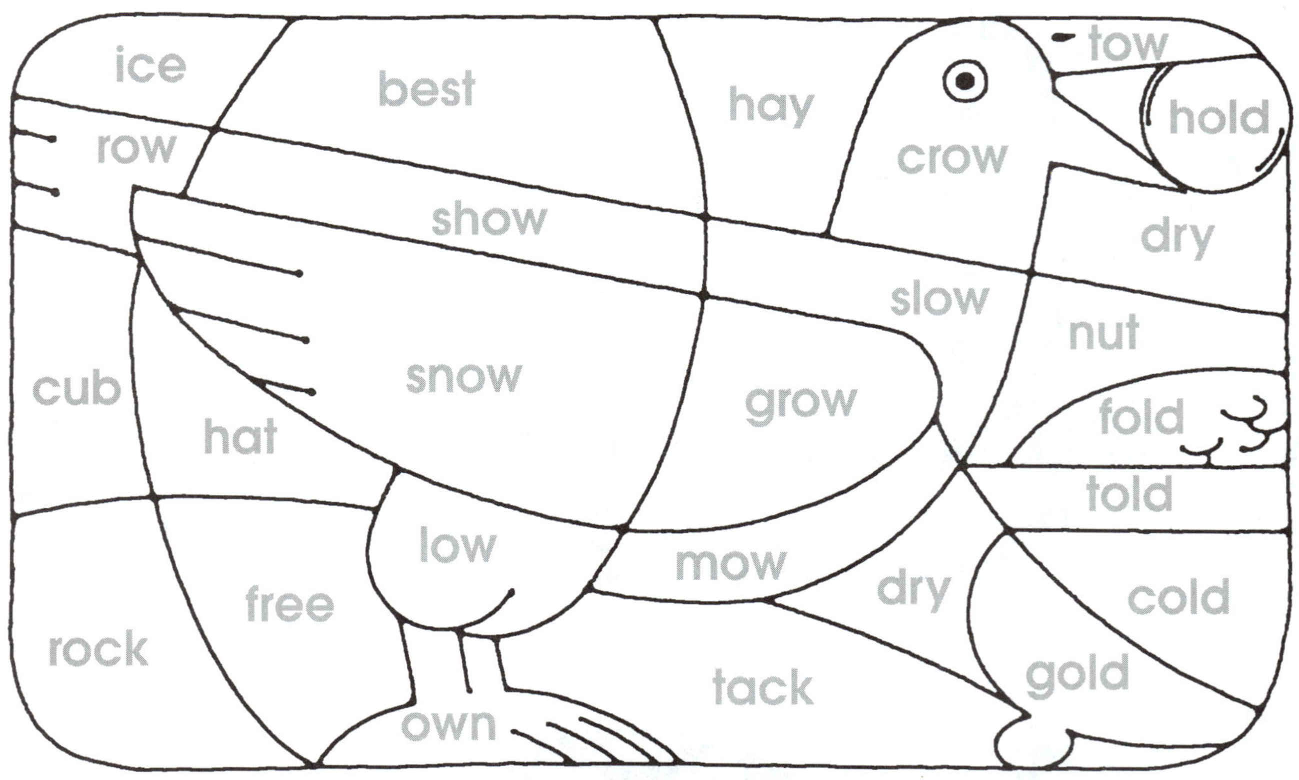

4. The two **long o** pictures are ____________ and ____________.

Write the **long o** words to finish the sentences.

show gold toad boat told go

1. The king's crown is made of ___________.

2. The knight ___________ us about the dragon.

3. The princess refused to kiss the ___________.

4. The princess does not want to ___________ home.

5. The knight used a ___________ to get to Dragon Island.

6. The jester put on a ___________ for the king.

WORDS WITH LONG o

Write the **long o** words that fit these shapes.
Then draw lines from the **long o** words to their pictures.

globe rope boat home goat gold

1.

2.

3.

4.

5.

6.

The Great Longo has a secret message for you!

1. Color the **long o** words blue.

2. The Great Longo's secret message is: ______________.

WORDS WITH LONG o

Help! The words got all mixed up.
Write the **long o** words for the pictures.

toad road goat hole rose globe

1. hoel

2. orad

3. toda

4. eosr

5. oatg

6. elobg

WORDS WITH LONG u

These words have the **long u** sound in .

cube cute huge
rule mule tube

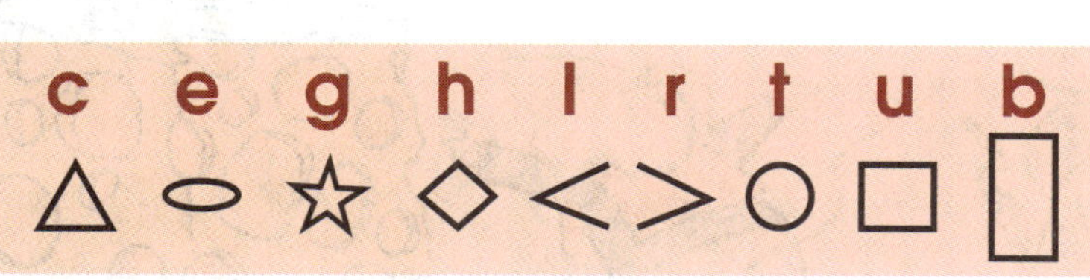

c	e	g	h	l	r	t	u	b
△	⬭	☆	◇	<	>	○	□	▯

Use the code to write the **long u** words.

1. △ □ ○ ⬭

2. ○ □ ▯ ⬭

3. ◇ □ ☆ ⬭

4. > □ < ⬭

Write the **long u** words for the pictures.

5. 

6. 

WORDS WITH LONG u

The letters **ew**, **u-e**, **ue**, and **ui** make the **long u** sound.

Use the **long u** letter combinations to finish the words.
Then write the whole words on the lines.

1. **ew**

n ___ ___ __________

d ___ ___ __________

bl ___ ___ __________

2. **u-e**

h___ g ___ __________

c___ b ___ __________

t ___ b ___ __________

3. **ue**

gl ___ ___ __________

d ___ ___ __________

bl ___ ___ __________

4. **ui**

fr___ ___t __________

j___ ___ce __________

s ___ ___t __________

Write the **long u** words to finish the sentences.

use	tube	cute
huge	glue	blue

1. An elephant is a ____________ animal.

2. We had to squeeze the ____________ hard to get the glue out.

3. The baby elephant got covered in sticky ____________.

4. The elephant had to ____________ lots of soap to get clean.

5. The water was bright ____________.

6. I thought the baby elephant was very ____________.

WORDS WITH LONG u

Draw lines from the pictures to the words.
Then write the **long u** words.

1.

2. 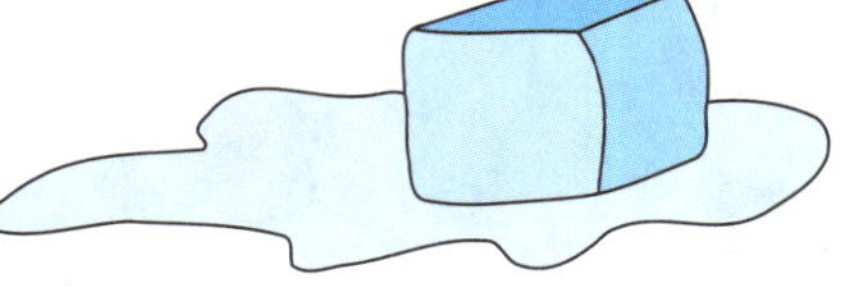

3. 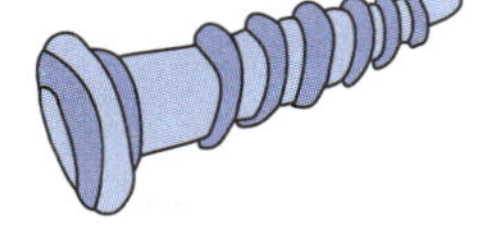

4. 

5. 

6. 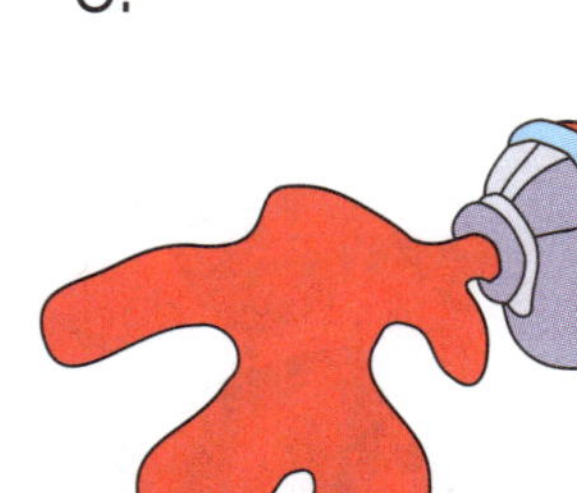

cube ______

fuel ______

glue ______

screw ______

tube ______

suit ______

1. Color the **long u** words **red**.

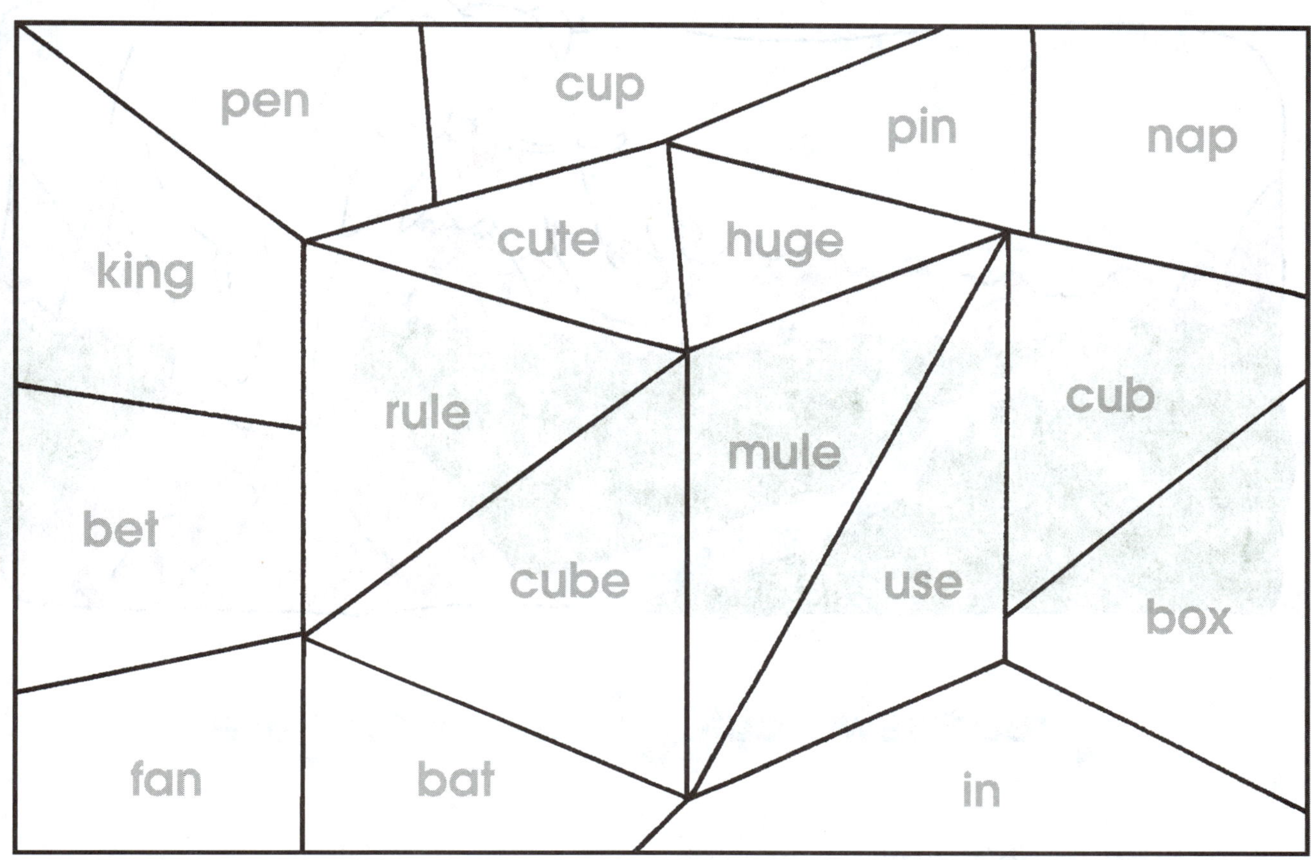

2. Write the **long u** words.

WORDS WITH LONG u

Write the **long u** words to finish the sentences.

true few cute huge view use

1. If there aren't many, there are ____________.

2. If it is not false, it is ____________.

3. I thought the baby was very ____________.

4. An elephant is a ____________ animal.

5. Standing on a mountain, you have a nice ____________.

6. When you work with something, you ____________ it.

Many words with a **long vowel sound** are spelled with **vowel-consonant-e**.

Add **e** to the words to make **long vowel** words.

1. at ___ 2. kit ___ 3. pin ___

4. hug ___ 5. dim ___ 6. mad ___

Help fly the kites.
Write the words from above on the correct kites.

9. It cost a ____________.

7. A whale is ____________.

8. It ____________ a mess.

10. How high can your ____________ fly?

11. That is a ____________ tree.

12. We ____________ pizza for lunch.

VOWEL - CONSONANT - E

As you've learned, many words with a **long vowel sound** are spelled with **vowel-consonant-e**. Here are some more:

cake bike rose cube

Write the **long vowel** words with the sounds.
Draw pictures for the **long vowel** words.

kite home tube rake

1. Long a

2. Long i

3. Long o

4. Long u

Write the **long vowel** words in the puzzle.

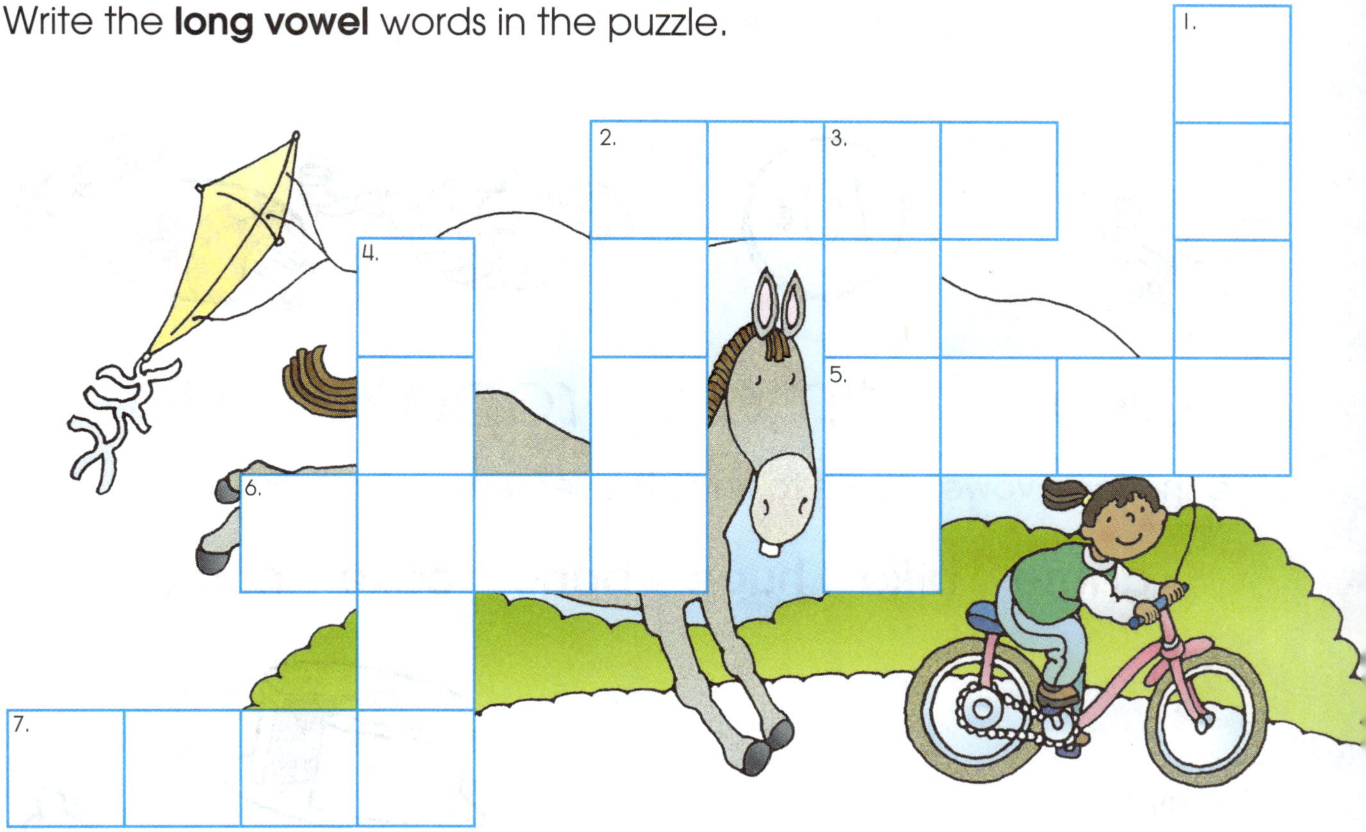

1. 2. 3. 4. 5. 6. 7.

Across

2.

5.

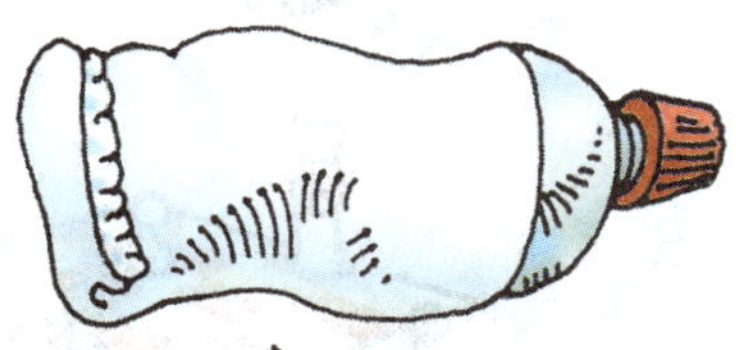

6.

7.

Down

1.

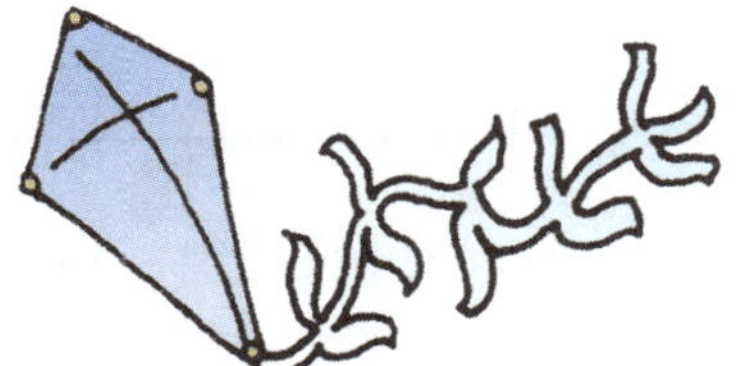

2.

3.

4.

Underline the **vowels** and **e** endings in the words.

rake dime rope tube

Write the **long vowel** words to finish the sentences.

game bike huge bone cake home

1. Amy made a ____________.

2. Give the dog a ____________.

3. I can ride a ____________.

4. Let's play a ____________.

5. Mom is at ____________.

6. An elephant is ____________.

Write the **long vowel** words for the clues.
Then read the letters in the box to answer the riddle.

home dime pine those
nine cute save make

1. keep ___ ___ ___ ___
2. pretty ___ ___ ___ ___
3. one more than eight ___ ___ ___ ___
4. plural of that ___ ___ ___ ___ ___
5. where a person lives ___ ___ ___ ___
6. a 10¢ coin ___ ___ ___ ___
7. a kind of tree ___ ___ ___ ___
8. build ___ ___ ___ ___

9. I brighten your day. What am I? ______________

Add the missing letters to make the **long vowel** words from the word list.

10. c___t___ 11. s___v___ 12. h___m___ 13. m___k___

14. d___m___ 15. th___s___ 16. n___n___ 17. p___n___

REVIEW: LONG VOWELS

Help! The words got all mixed up.
Write the **long vowel** words for the pictures.

ape sheep icicle coat mule cube

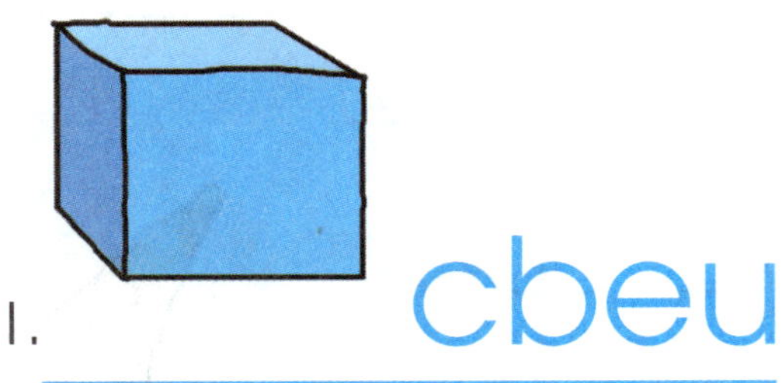

1. cbeu

2. elmu

3. spehe

4. eap

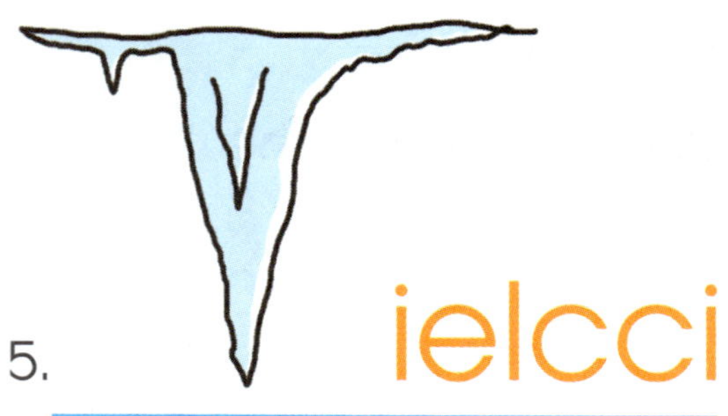

5. ielcci

6. aotc

Write the **long vowel** words that mean the **opposite** of:

take sleep low sweet dry clean
go white over cold me night

1. **dirty** ____________

2. **hot** ____________

3. **sour** ____________

4. **you** ____________

5. **black** ____________

6. **under** ____________

7. **day** ____________

8. **give** ____________

9. **wake** ____________

10. **wet** ____________

11. **come** ____________

12. **high** ____________

REVIEW: LONG VOWELS

Circle the correct spellings for the **long vowel** pictures.

1. **cake** **caek**
2. **beot** **beet**
3. **tie** **tyi**

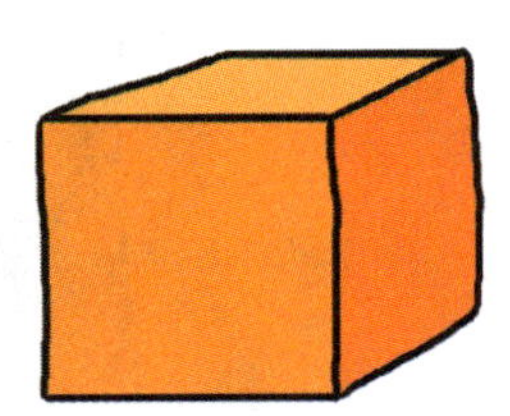

4. **bow** **boe**
5. **cobe** **cube**
6. **vace** **vase**

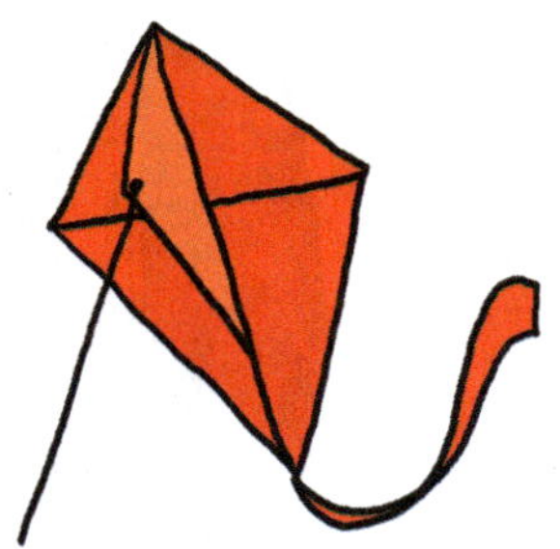
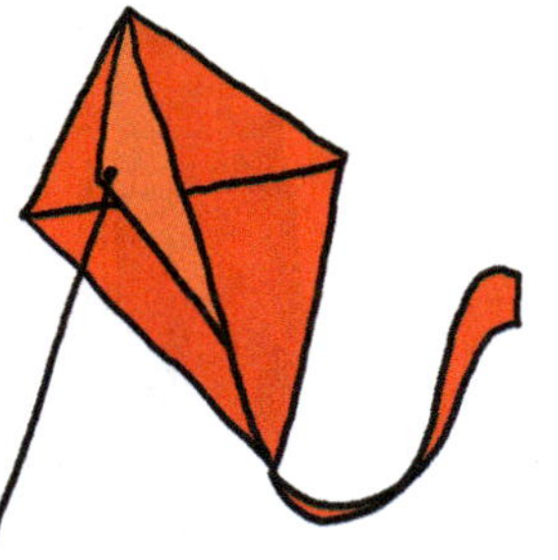

7. **bea** **bee**
8. **kite** **klet**
9. **rope** **roap**

10. **mule** **muel**
11. **tree** **tre**
12. **payl** **pail**

Help! The words got all mixed up.
Write the **long vowel** words for the pictures.

cane peas vine soap glue toad

1. tdao

2. cean

3. espa

4. einv

5. oaps

6. uelg

Read the clues.
Write the **long vowel** answers in the puzzle.

new rain play clean
light dime honey boat

1. 2. 3. 4. 5. 6. 7. 8.

Across

2. equal to ten pennies
4. a small ship
6. You _____ an instrument.
7. drops of water from clouds

Down

1. not heavy
3. food made by bees
5. free from dirt
8. never used

The Great Longo is playing **long vowel** opposites. You can play, too!
Write the **long vowel** words that mean the **opposite** of:

right like old die
no day fake mine
over keep same sleep

1. **left** ____________
2. **dislike** ____________
3. **below** ____________
4. **night** ____________
5. **give** ____________
6. **yes** ____________
7. **different** ____________
8. **real** ____________
9. **yours** ____________
10. **live** ____________
11. **wake** ____________
12. **new** ____________

Write the **long vowel** words for the pictures.
Draw lines from the words to the **long vowel** sounds you hear.

goat nine sheep cane cube

1. ______________________

Long a

2. ______________________

Long e

9

3. ______________________

Long i

Long o

4. ______________________

Long u

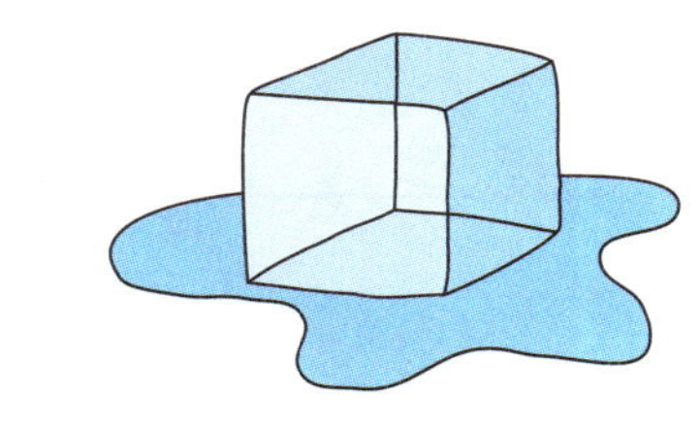

5. ______________________

The Great Longo has another secret message for you!

1. Color the **long vowel** words **green**.

thumb bun dance
fog log had
bet jump
sit clock run set pet
know thief cake
nice ice no
let if lit
rice
go hike hill
pie at
cute seen glue rake say mean
sock had met
net hit dog
bit
jog not sun
fun
has mad

2. The Great Longo's secret message is: ____________.

Write five sentences using one of these **long vowel** words in each sentence.

me
like
cute
home
game

1.

2.

3.

4.

5.

Write the **long vowel** words that mean the **opposite** of:

dry
over
clean
sleep
cold
low
go
me
sweet
white
night

1. **dirty** ____________
2. **you** ____________
3. **day** ____________
4. **black** ____________
5. **hot** ____________
6. **wet** ____________
7. **wake** ____________
8. **under** ____________
9. **sour** ____________
10. **high** ____________
11. **come** ____________

REVIEW: LONG VOWELS

Write the **long vowel** words for the pictures.

peas mule five rain bee home light rope

1.

2. 

3. 

4. 

5. 

6. 

7. 

8. 

REVIEW: LONG VOWELS

Write the **long vowel** words to finish the sentences.

same jeans know money time snails coat cube

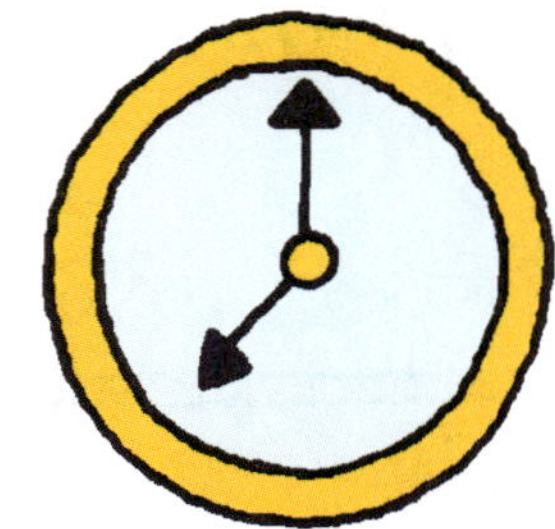

1. A clock tells ____________ .

2. I ____________ the answer.

3. We have the ____________ first name.

4. My dirty ____________ need to be washed.

5. Wear your warmest ____________ today.

6. A ____________ has six sides.

7. ____________ move very slowly.

8. How much ____________ does the ticket cost?

WORDS WITH a, ai, ay

Finish the **a**, **ai**, and **ay** words by filling in the missing letters.

Add the missing letters to finish the sentences.

9. Did your mom s___ ___ you could pl___ ___?

10. Can you st___ ___ all d___ ___?

11. Do not w___ ___t in the r___ ___n.

WORDS WITH o, oa, ow

Write the **o**, **oa**, and **ow** words for the clues.
Then read the letters in the box to answer the riddle.

own told show both coat grow goat

1. get bigger ___ ___ ___ ___

2. worn over clothes ___ ___ ___ ___

3. put in sight ___ ___ ___ ___

4. one, then another ___ ___ ___ ___

5. have ___ ___ ___

6. a farm animal ___ ___ ___ ___

7. said; put into words ___ ___ ___ ___

8. I float on water.
What am I?

a ______________________

Add the missing letters to make the **o**, **oa**, and **ow** words from the word list.

9. gr___ ___ 10. sh___ ___ 11. ___wn 12. t___ld

13. c___ ___t 14. b___th 15. g___ ___t

WORDS ENDING WITH y

The letter **y** has an **e** sound at the end of some words.
Read the clues.
Write the **y** answers in the puzzle.

penny **kitty** **pretty** **easy**
silly **lucky** **funny** **baby**

1.
2.
3.
4.
5.
6.
7.
8.

Across

3. causing laughter
5. not hard
7. foolish
8. very young child

Down

1. cute
2. having good luck
4. one cent
6. baby cat

WORDS ENDING WITH y

Write the **y** words to finish the sentences.

kitty happy story baby easy silly penny party

1. Molly has a new __________ sister.

2. I was __________ to be home again.

3. We named our __________ Socks.

4. Maisy invited me to her birthday __________.

5. I need one more __________ to make five cents.

6. Dad read me a __________ about pirates.

7. The math test was __________.

8. Goober is a __________ name.

Brent made a talking machine at school.
It makes **br** words.
Find the words the machine made.
Write the **br** words on the blanks.

____

____

____

____

____

____

Help! The words got all mixed up.
Write the **cr** words for the pictures.

cry
crab
crow
crate
crown
crayon
cricket

1.  wrocn

2.  rcy

3.  yracon

4. 

acert

5. arcb

6.  wcor

7.  reckcit

Write the **dr** words to finish the sentences.

driver dragon dress drip
drink draw drum dry

1. Take a ____________ of water.

2. The bus ____________ was late.

3. If it is not shut off, the faucet will ____________ .

4. My sister was wearing a beautiful ____________ .

5. The ____________ was green and purple.

6. I like to practice playing the ____________ .

7. It takes a long time to ____________ my hair.

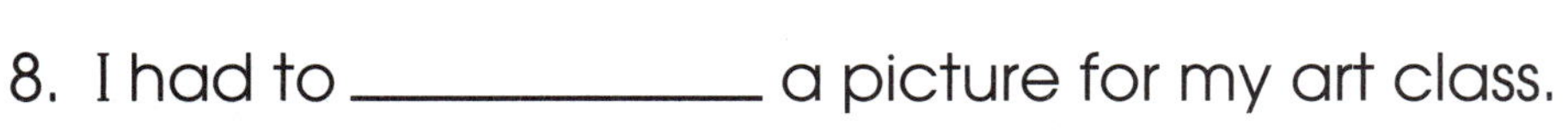

8. I had to ____________ a picture for my art class.

This is Flora's first day of school.
Read the clues.
Write the **fl** answers in the puzzle.

flower fly floor flame flute flag

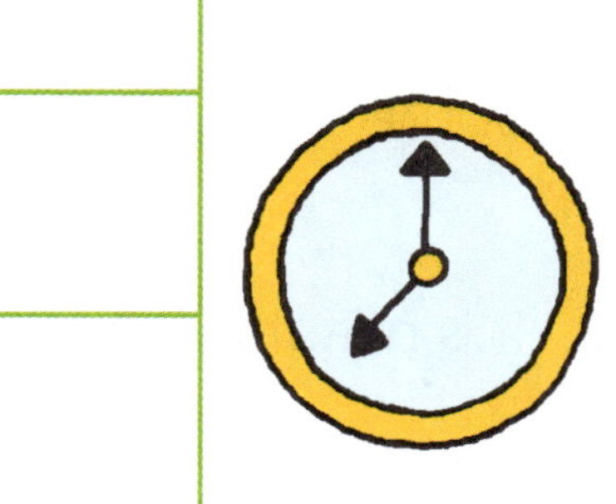

Across

1. an insect
2. We stand on it.
3. It can make music.

Down

1. A rose is a ____ .
2. light given off from fire
3. All countries have a ____ .

Frances is helping Fred learn **fr** words.
Write the **fr** words to finish the sentences.

frog	front	from
fruit	friend	free

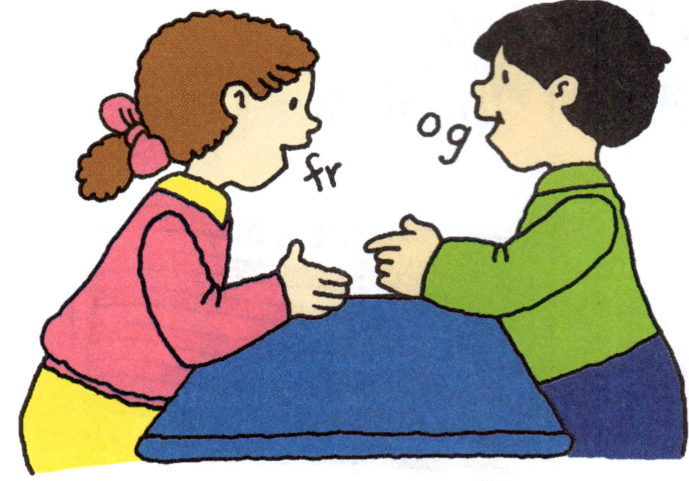

1. Someone you like is a ____________.

2. It is not the back. It is the ____________.

3. Maria got a present ____________ Jimmy.

4. A ____________ is a green animal that hops.

5. Bananas are a ____________ and so are apples.

6. We rode every ride because the tickets were ____________.

Greg had to write a paper about himself.
What did Greg write?
Write the **gr** words to finish the story.

group	grape	growl	grunt
grass	grow	green	Greg

My name is __________. I like to play outside on the

__________ __________. Sometimes I pretend to

be a monster, and I __________ and __________.

I play monster with a __________ of friends.

Then Mom makes peanut butter and __________ jelly

sandwiches for us. Even monsters need food to __________!

Write **pr** on the blanks to spell the words. Then connect the dots from 1 to 6 to see what Priscilla's classmates will give her.

1. ___ ___etty

6. ___ ___ize

2. ___ ___ess

5. ___ ___ince

3. ___ ___oud

4. ___ ___esent

Priscilla's classmates will give her a ______________.

Write the **sl** words on the slide.
Write the **pl** words on the plane.

sled slam please slice sleep
plant slip planet plane plate

BLENDS: sm, sn

Sam's snail is on his way to school.
Help Sam follow his trail.
Write the **sm** and **sn** words by the pictures.

Spencer and Swain are at a swim meet.
Help them stay in their lanes.
Write the **sp** words on Spencer's side and the **sw** words on Swain's side.

sweet spot swim spider
spring swan spoon swing

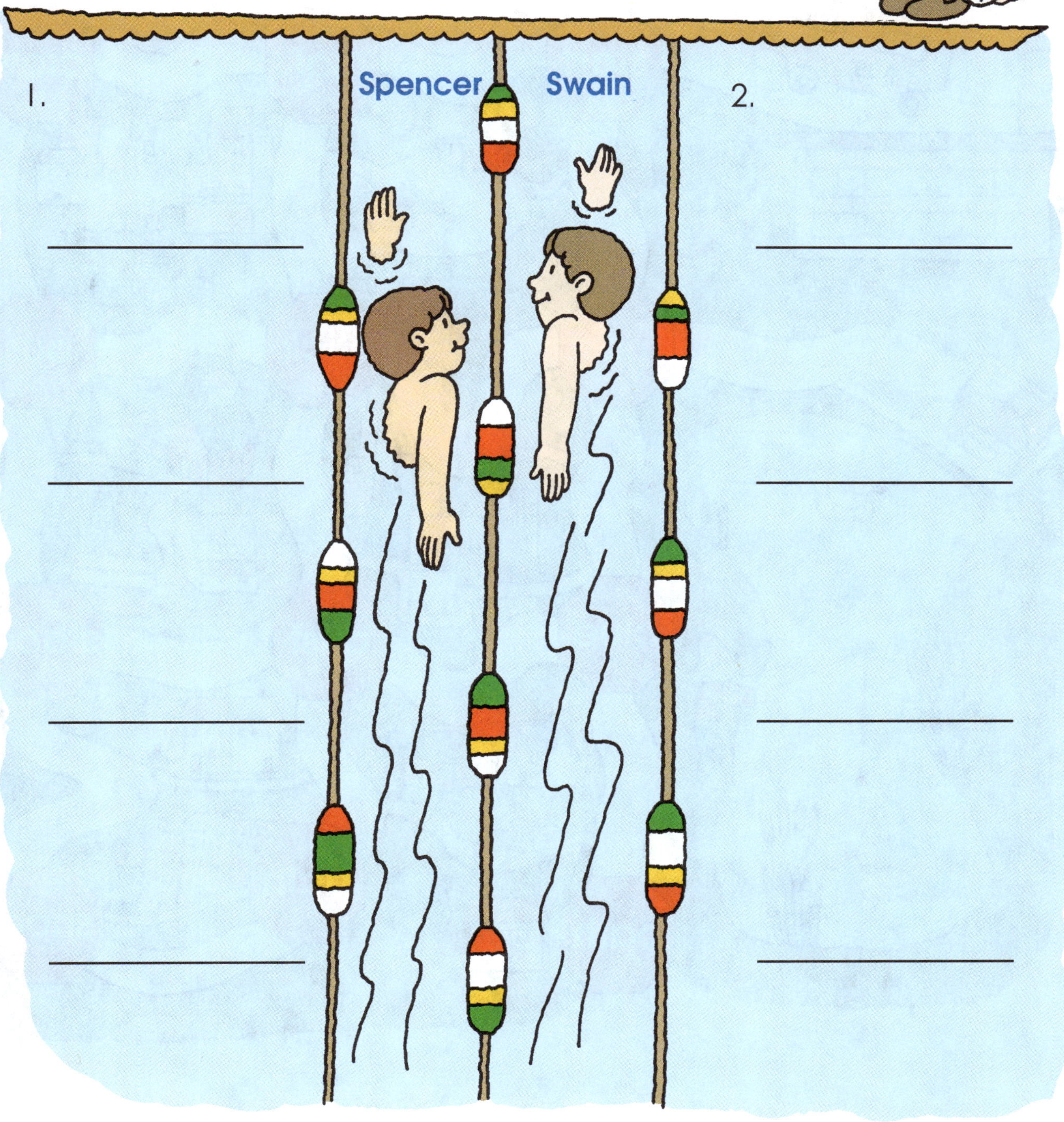

Spencer Swain

1. ____________
____
____
____

2. ____________
____
____
____

The class is taking a trip. Help them find the zoo.
Follow the path of **st** words.
The words may **begin** or **end** with **st**.

bee
dish
shell
fox
store
best
last
just
stir
snap
food
boy
sun
ZOO

BLENDS: spr, str

It is show and tell time at school. What will Jill tell?
Write the **spr** and **str** words to finish the story.

street	strawberry	spray
stream	sprinkler	spring

Dad had to water the new__________ plants. He put the __________ by the plants. Then he turned on the water. A big __________ of water shot into the air. It began to make a long __________ down the __________. Dad had to fix a bad __________. Now we have lots of juicy berries to share.

BLEND: tr

tr

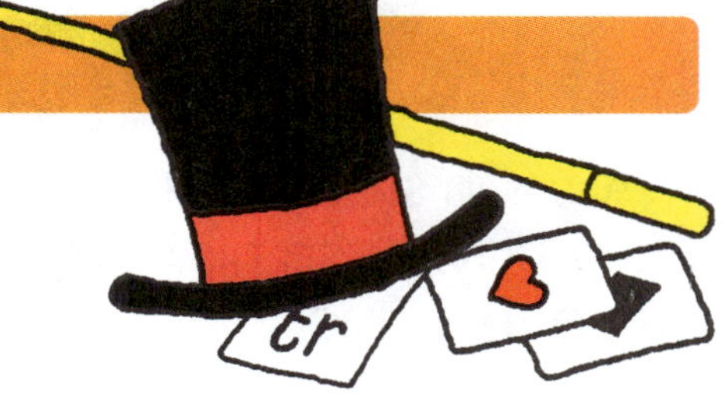

Trina is trying to trick Trent.
She made a **tr** puzzle.
Write **tr** on the blanks to spell the words.

1. ___ ___actor
2. ___ ___ee
3. ___ ___ick
4. ___ ___ain
5. ___ ___y
6. ___ ___ip
7. ___ ___uck
8. ___ ___ap
9. ___ ___ue

10. Circle the **tr** words in the word search.

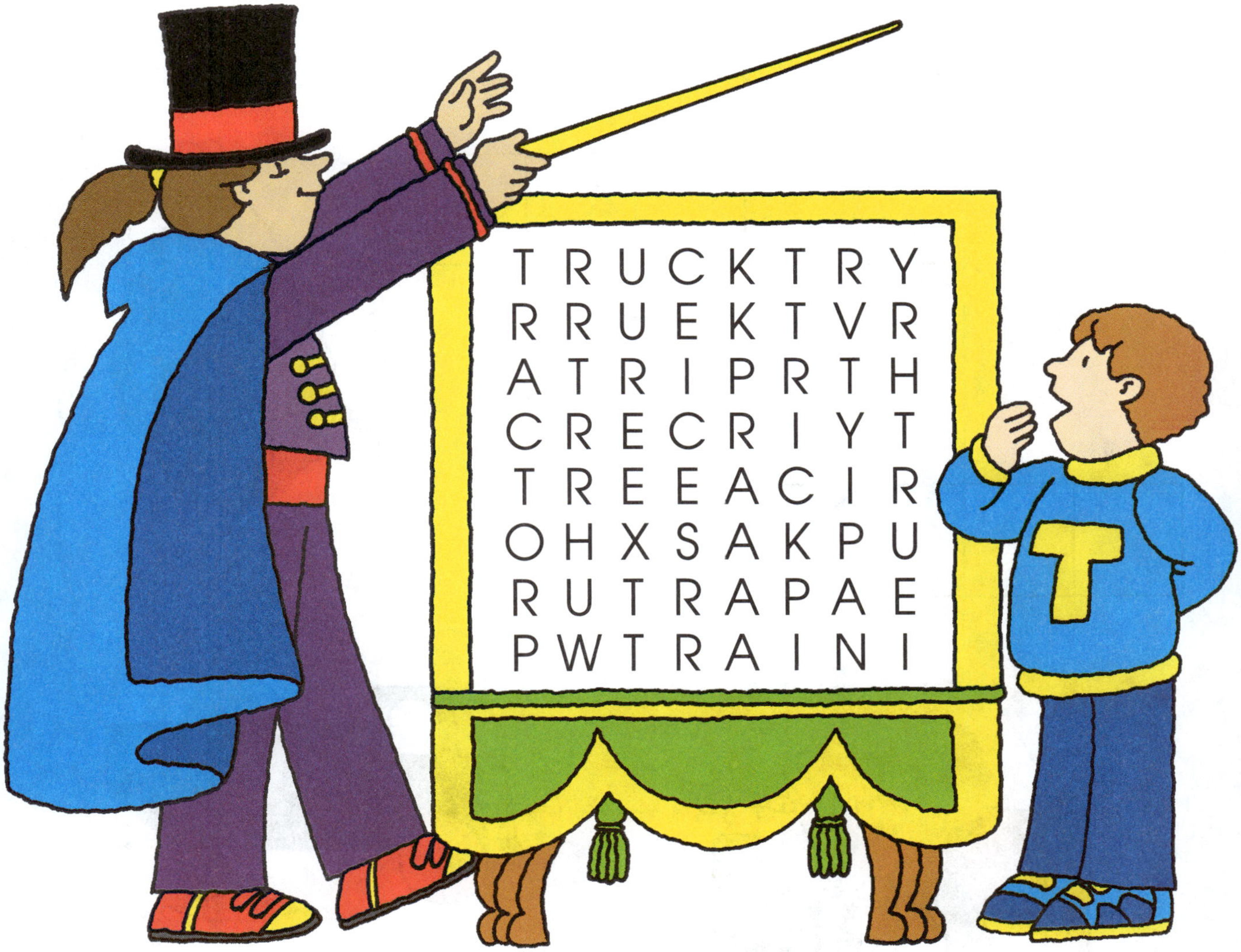
T R U C K T R Y
R R U E K T V R
A T R I P R T H
C R E C R I Y T
T R E E A C I R
O H X S A K P U
R U T R A P A E
P W T R A I N I
T

Travis is in study hall.
Help Travis with his homework.
Read the clues.
Write the **tr** answers in the puzzle.

true trap truck
tree trip trick

Across

2. What rhymes with slip?
3. What rhymes with luck?
4. What rhymes with bee?

Down

1. What rhymes with clap?
2. What rhymes with stick?
3. What rhymes with blue?

1.

2.

3.

4.

REVIEW: BLENDS

Clara forget to finish the blend words.
Write the letters to spell the **blend** words.

ue ee ib ock ink
ag og ot ove owman

1. bl___ ___

2. fr___ ___

3. sp___ ___

4. tr___ ___

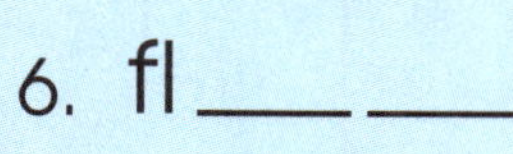

5. gl___ ___ ___

6. fl___ ___

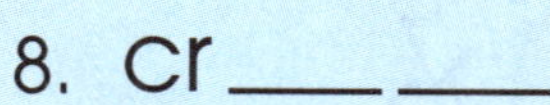

7. cl___ ___ ___

8. cr___ ___

9. dr___ ___ ___

10. sn___ ___ ___ ___ ___

Brent has homework to do.
Help Brent finish the puzzle.
Read the clues.
Write the **blend** answers in the puzzle.

Jack	click	brown
crack	blank	clown

Across

2. fill in the ________
3. a funny person
4. a break

Down

1. a name
2. a color
3. a sound

1.

2.

3.

4.

The children have their mittens mixed up.
Draw lines to show which mittens go together and make **blend** words.

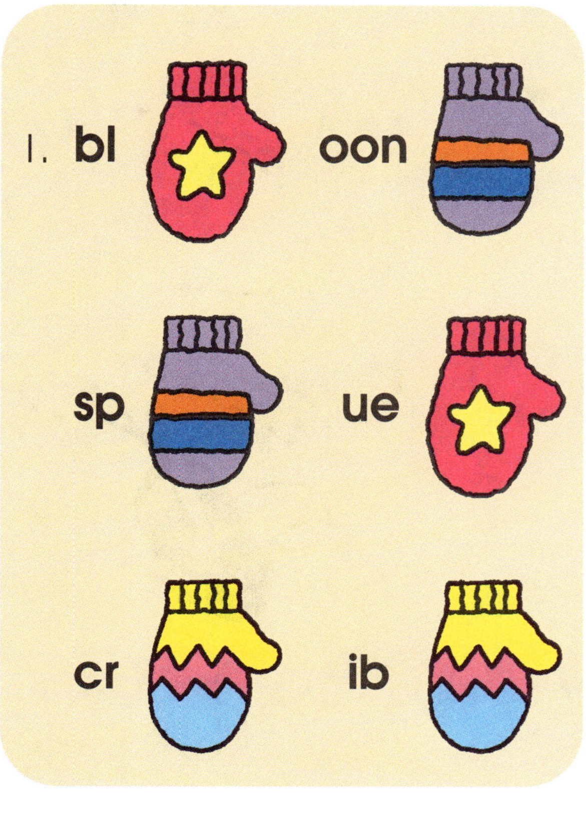

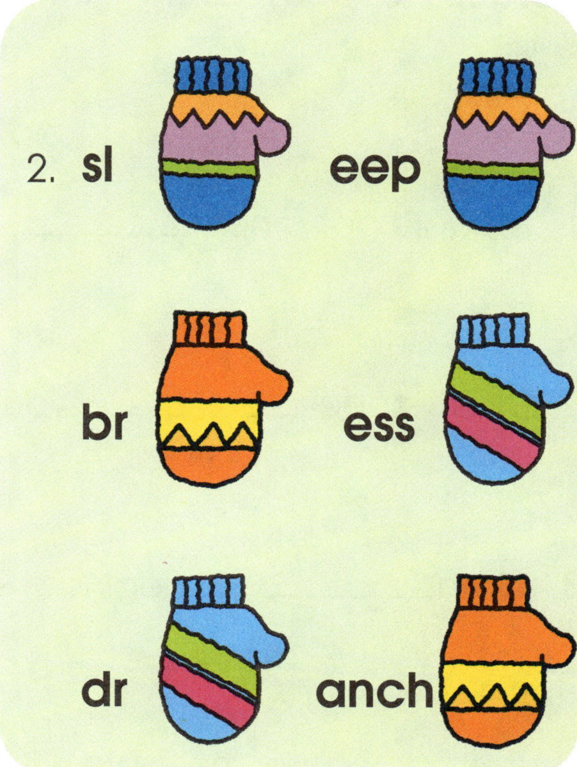

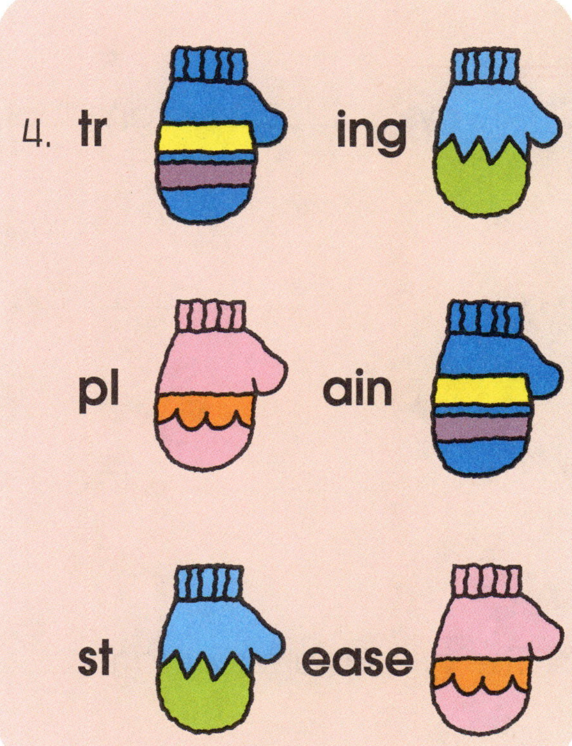

Write the **blend** words to finish the sentences.

class dress drag sting sweet smile smell stop

1. Maggie got a new __________ for her birthday.

2. Did the bee __________ you?

3. Math __________ begins at 9:00.

4. The baby gave me a big __________.

5. Always __________ and look before you cross a street.

6. Dad had to __________ the box to the car.

7. I like to __________ pizza baking.

8. The grapes are nice and __________.

Take a test with the class.
Fill in the blanks with the correct **s blends** to spell the words.

Name: ______________________

1. **str** **sl**

___ ___ ___awberry

2. **sl** **sn**

___ ___ail

3. **sw** **st**

___ ___an

4. **spr** **str**

___ ___ ___inkler

5. **sm** **st**

___ ___ing

6. **sl** **sm**

___ ___ile

7. **sw** **st**

___ ___eet

8. **sl** **st**

___ ___ar

It is Fun Day at recess. The students are on a treasure hunt. What will they find? Write the correct **blend** words by the pictures. Start at the bottom of the page.

grapes prize crow
frog bread dragon tree

REVIEW: BLENDS

Spell **blend** words by adding the **bold** endings.

1.	gr**ay**	M ___ ___	tr ___ ___	pl ___ ___
2.	cr**y**	fr ___	fl ___	sk ___
3.	dr**ip**	fl ___ ___	sl ___ ___	sk ___ ___
4.	gr**ow**	bl ___ ___	cr ___ ___	sl ___ ___
5.	br**own**	dr ___ ___ ___	fr ___ ___ ___	cl ___ ___ ___
6.	sk**ill**	sp ___ ___ ___	st ___ ___ ___	gr ___ ___ ___
7.	cr**ack**	tr ___ ___ ___	bl ___ ___ ___	st ___ ___ ___
8.	br**ing**	cl ___ ___ ___	fl ___ ___ ___	st ___ ___ ___

1. Color the **r blends** green.

br fr pr gr dr cr tr

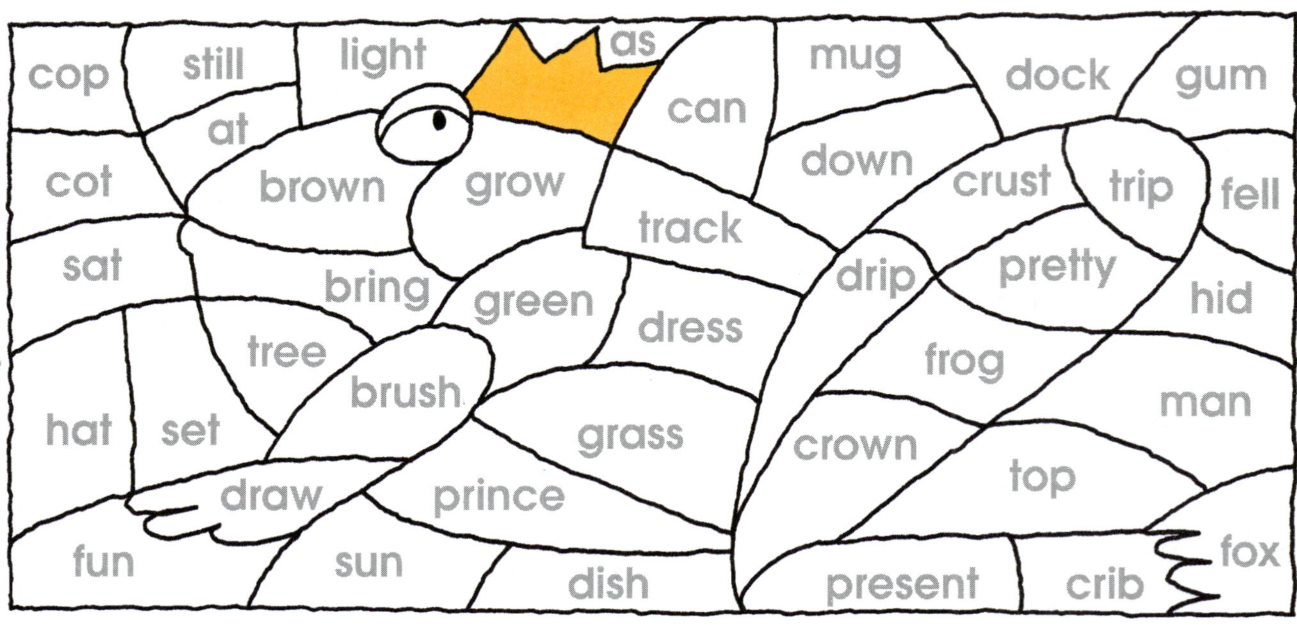

2. Choose **blend** words from the picture to fill in the blanks below.

pr word ______________

fr word ______________

br word ______________

tr word ______________

gr word ______________

cr word ______________

dr word ______________

REVIEW: BLENDS

Use the **l blends** to finish the words.

1. **bl**

___ ___ ock

___ ___ ue

___ ___ ink

2. **gl**

___ ___ ad

___ ___ obe

___ ___ itter

3. **cl**

___ ___ own

___ ___ ock

___ ___ ub

4. **pl**

___ ___ an

___ ___ ay

___ ___ us

5. **fl**

___ ___ ower

___ ___ ag

___ ___ y

6. **sl**

___ ___ ip

___ ___ eep

___ ___ ow

7. Find the **l blend** words in the word search.

B	L	I	N	K	B	L	O	C	K	G	S	G
P	L	U	S	S	L	I	P	L	F	L	D	L
C	L	U	B	W	U	R	N	O	D	A	U	O
N	S	K	I	C	E	N	A	W	L	D	P	B
F	L	A	G	S	L	O	W	N	T	S	L	E
L	E	O	C	P	C	L	O	C	K	E	A	G
Y	E	B	G	L	I	T	T	E	R	O	Y	T
T	P	L	A	N	L	F	L	O	W	E	R	F

Today, Glen came to our class.
Learn more about Glen.
Write the **blend** words to finish the story.

glides Glen clear blue globe
flies plane clouds black sleeps

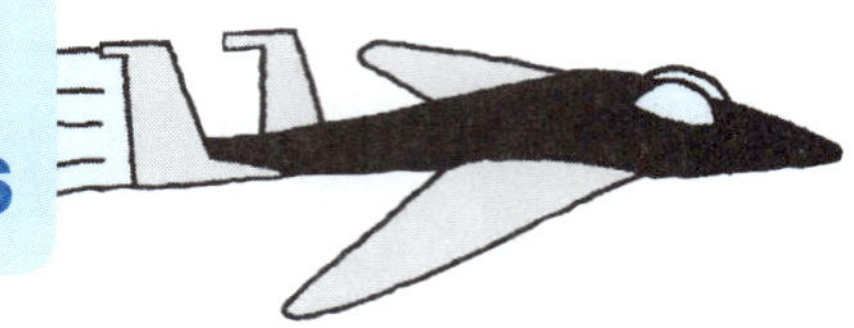

1. ____________ is a pilot. His ____________ is silver and ____________ .

He ____________ high in the ____________, ____________ sky. He

____________ above the ____________. He goes around the

____________. When he ____________, nobody knows.

2. Find out where Glen landed.
Put an X in the box by the state whose name begins with a **blend**.

☐ Ohio ☐ Florida ☐ Maine

Help the class do a blend puzzle.
Read the clues.
Write the **bl**, **cl**, and **gl** answers in the puzzle.

blue clock clean glue
blocks cloud glad glove
black clothes globe

Across

2. opposite of white
4. holds things together
5. a form of moisture in the sky
7. building toys
9. a round map
10. opposite of dirty

Down

1. what we wear
3. keeps time
4. happy
6. worn on the hand
8. color of the sky

Use the **s blends** to finish the words.

1. **sk** ___ ___in
   ___ ___ip
2. **sh** ___ ___ape
   ___ ___ell
3. **sp** ___ ___eed
   ___ ___ill
4. **st** ___ ___ory
   ___ ___amp
5. **sl** ___ ___eep
   ___ ___ime
6. **sn** ___ ___ap
   ___ ___ail
7. **sm** ___ ___oke
   ___ ___all
8. **sw** ___ ___eet
   ___ ___im

9. Complete the story with **s blend** words from above.

This is a st__ __ __of a sm__ __ __ sn__ __ __named Sk__ __.

Sk__ __lives in a curly sh __ __ __. His sk__ __feels like sl__ __e.

Sp__ __ __ does not matter to him. If he is in danger, he goes into

his sh__ __ __. He also goes into his sh__ __ __to sl__ __ __.

Sw__ __ __dreams, Sk __ __!

COMBINATION SOUND: ch

Chad and Mitch have a **ch** project.
They need objects with the **ch** sound.
Draw lines from the words that **start** with **ch** to **Chad**.
Draw lines from the words that **end** with **ch** to **Mitch**.

cheese	**bird**
porch	**chimney**
cow	**bear**
dog	**catch**
chair	**match**
banana	**book**
smile	**glass**
watch	**cherry**
fish	**man**

Chad

Mitch

COMBINATION SOUND: sh

The class took an **sh** field trip.
They went to a sheep farm and a fish farm.
Write the words that **start** with **sh** in the sheep pen.
Write the words that **end** with **sh** in the fish pond.

push	shop	shoe
show	dish	shirt
shell	wash	wish

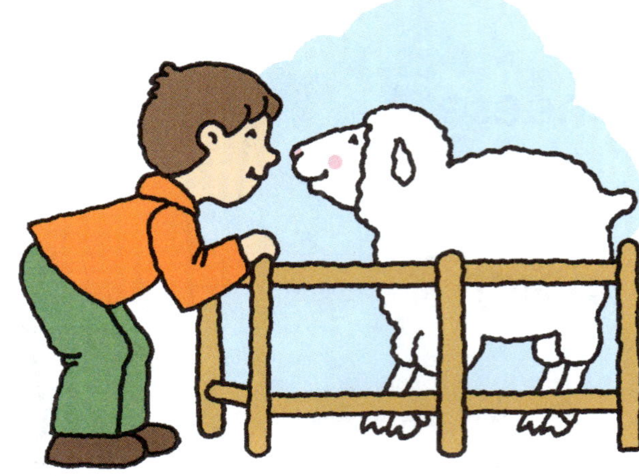

1.

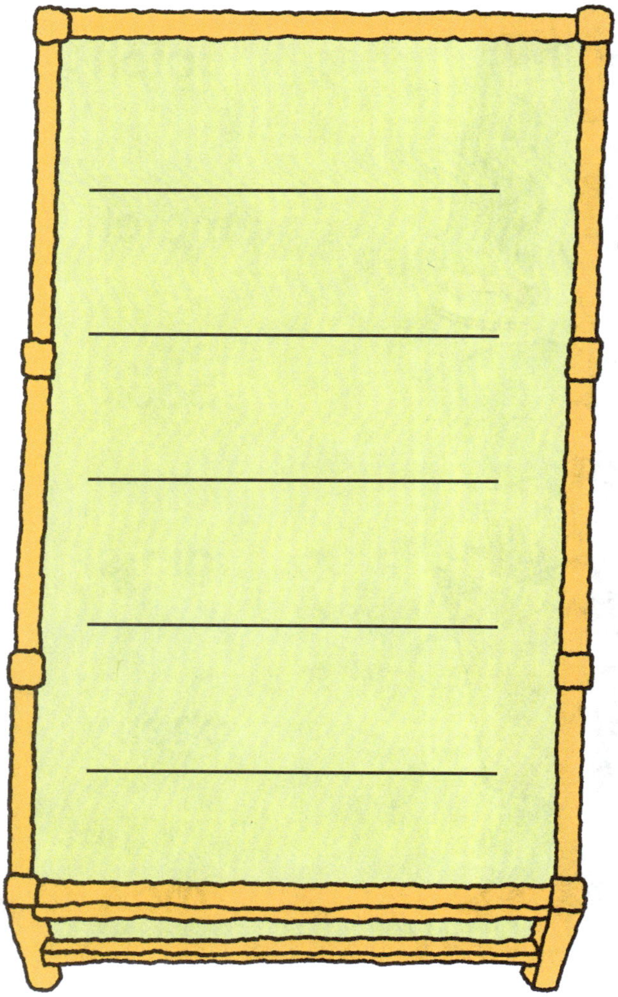

2.

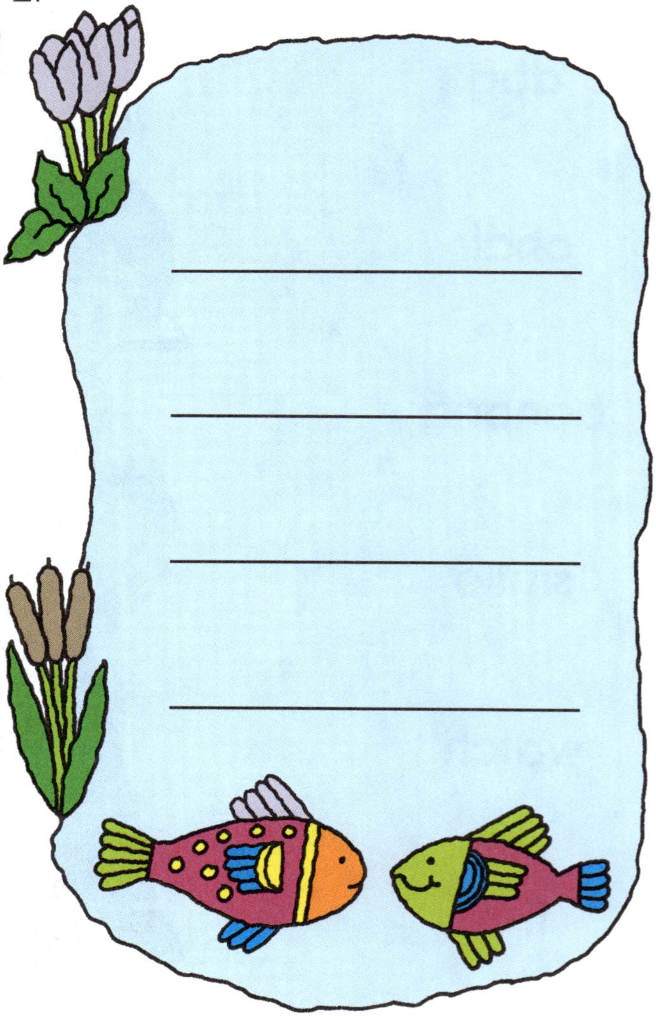

Help Thelma and Meredith write a paper.
Write the **th** words to finish the story.

bath	path
there	Thank
thirty	think

Our dog, Rex, would not let us give him a ____________.

We____________ he's afraid of water. Rex tried to run from us, but

we followed his ____________. It took us almost ____________

minutes to catch him. ____________ goodness Mom was

____________ to help us.

It is summer vacation. Keep your skills sharp. Write the missing letters to finish the words that end with **ch**, **sh**, and **th** sounds.

1. **ch**

mat___ ___

chur___ ___

wat___ ___

por___ ___

2. **sh**

wa___ ___

pu___ ___

di___ ___

3. **th**

mou___ ___

sou___ ___

pa___ ___

ba___ ___

4. Find the words in the word search.

COMBINATION SOUNDS: ch, sh, th

Write the missing letters to finish the words that end with **ch**, **sh**, and **th** sounds.

1. **ch**	2. **sh**	3. **th**
tea ___ ___	fi ___ ___	tee ___ ___
bea ___ ___	ru ___ ___	clo ___ ___
rea ___ ___	wi ___ ___	mo ___ ___
pea ___ ___	di ___ ___	bo ___ ___

4. Find the words in the word search.

T	I	Q	B	E	A	C	H	B
E	R	U	S	H	Q	W	P	O
A	T	E	E	T	H	I	E	T
C	M	O	T	H	X	S	A	H
H	C	L	O	T	H	H	C	D
F	I	S	H	D	I	S	H	R
L	X	R	E	A	C	H	W	F

Mrs. White wants the class to learn how to whistle.
Help them whistle to all the **wh** words.

Write **wh** on the blanks to spell the words.

1. ___ ___eel
2. ___ ___ y
3. ___ ___ en
4. ___ ___eat
5. ___ ___ ale
6. ___ ___ at
7. ___ ___istle
8. ___ ___ ite
9. ___ ___ ere

10. Circle the **wh** words in the word search.

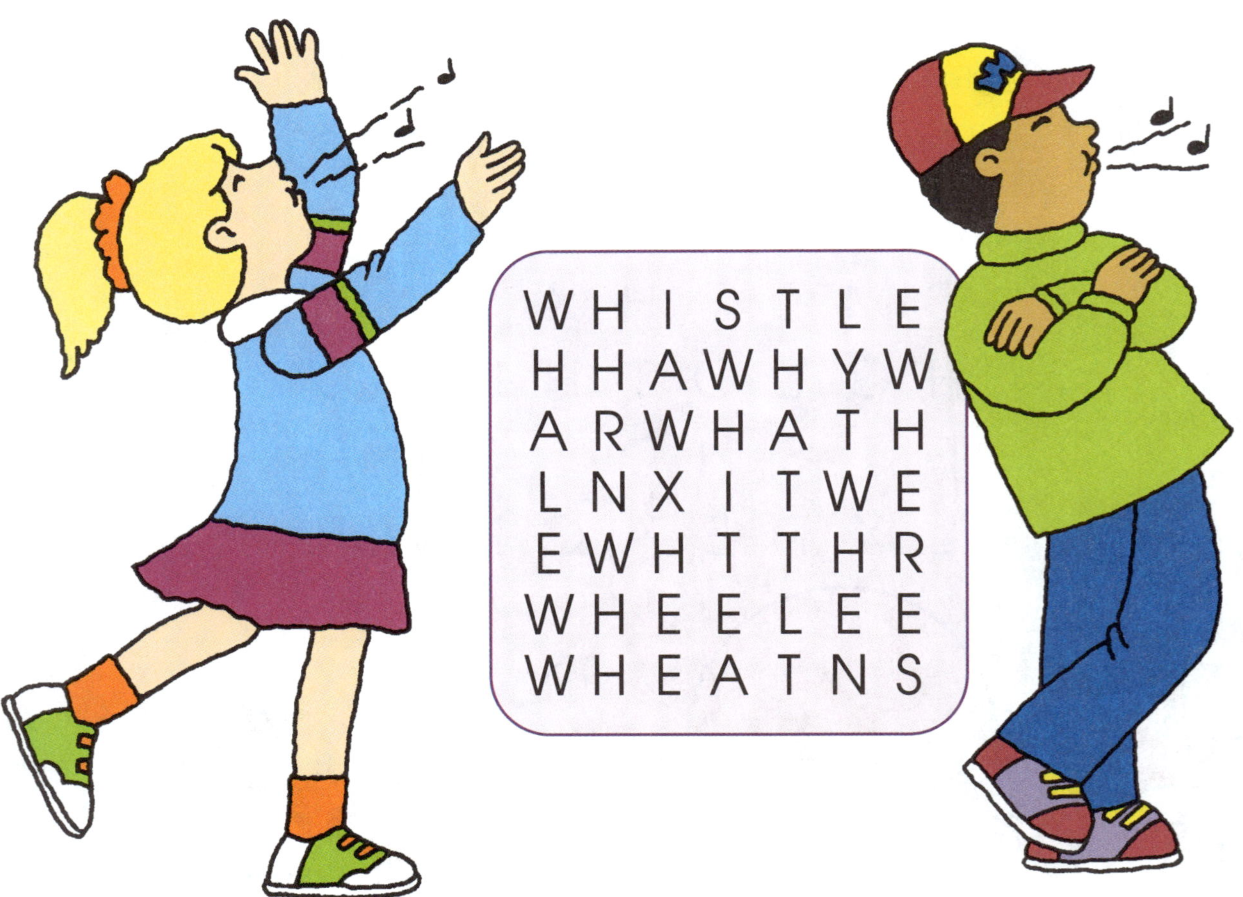

shell cherry third think
wheel whale ship chair

Write the words that **begin** like:

1. **ch**ild ____________ ____________

2. **th**ick ____________ ____________

3. **wh**ite ____________ ____________

4. **sh**op ____________ ____________

north watch fish

Write the words that **end** like:

5. ea**ch** ____________

6. ba**th** ____________

7. wa**sh** ____________

It is time for lunch. What is on the menu?
Write the missing letters on the blanks.

ch sh th wh

___ ___ ite milk

___ ___ eat bread

___ ___ icken sandwi ___ ___

bro ___ ___

___ ___ erry pie

soft ___ ___ ell tacos

School is over for the year.
What does Shelly find in her desk?
Write the **ch**, **sh**, **th**, and **wh** words on the lines.

shirt	dish	shoe
sheep	watch	three
whale	whistle	cherry
cheese	wheel	bathtub

1. ______________ 2. ______________

3. ______________ 4. ______________

5. ______________ 6. ______________

7. ______________ 8. ______________

9. ______________ 10. ______________

11. ______________ 12. ______________

COMBINATION SOUNDS: ch, sh, th, wh

Write the **combination sound** words to finish the sentences.

shell What ship thick sheep whale chicken third

1. A ____________ is a very big boat.

2. The blue ____________ is the largest animal.

3. I had ____________ soup for lunch.

4. Jan was ____________ in the race.

5. ____________ time is it?

6. The dog's fur is very ____________ .

7. The egg's ____________ is cracked.

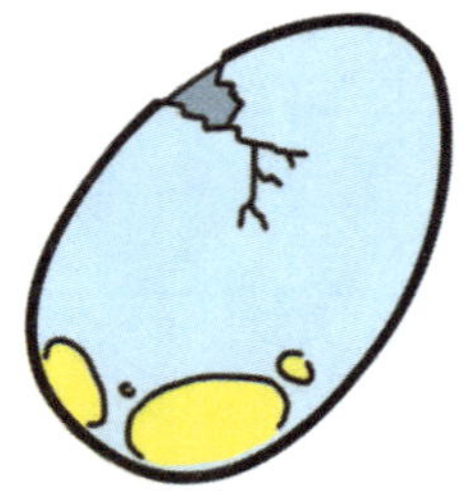

8. If you can't sleep, try counting ____________ .

Write the **er** words to finish the sentences.

after	over
flower	under
water	better
sister	answer

1. The ball went ____________ the chair.
2. It is your turn ____________ Sara.
3. May I have a drink of ____________?
4. A rose is a ____________.
5. Can you ____________ the question?
6. Her ____________ is six today.
7. Sara feels ____________ today.
8. The cat jumped ____________ the fence.
9. Circle the **er** words in the word search.

A	F	T	E	R	O	A
S	L	B	K	J	V	N
I	O	I	S	T	E	S
S	W	A	T	E	R	W
T	E	H	C	T	T	E
E	R	U	N	D	E	R
R	B	E	T	T	E	R

Read the clues.
Write the **combination sound** answers in the puzzle.

dirty	hurt	hurry	better
bird	third	turtle	every

Across

2. Ben ____ his finger in the door.
3. His finger feels ____ now.
4. Beth came in ____ place.
5. I pulled ____ weed in the garden.

Down

1. My shoes got ____ in the mud.
2. ____ or we will be late.
3. If an animal has feathers, it's a ____.
4. A ____ lives on land and in water.

COMBINATION SOUNDS: er, ir, ur

Write the **er**, **ir**, and **ur** words that **rhyme** with:

mother hurry letter nurse thirst bird dirty turn

1. **brother** ____________________
2. **first** ____________________
3. **purse** ____________________
4. **furry** ____________________
5. **thirty** ____________________
6. **third** ____________________
7. **burn** ____________________
8. **better** ____________________

Write three sentences using one of these **combination sound** words in each sentence.

girl surprise dinner

9. ____________________

10. ____________________

11. ____________________

COMBINATION SOUNDS: er, ir, ur

Read the clues.
Write the **er**, **ir**, and **ur** answers in the puzzle.

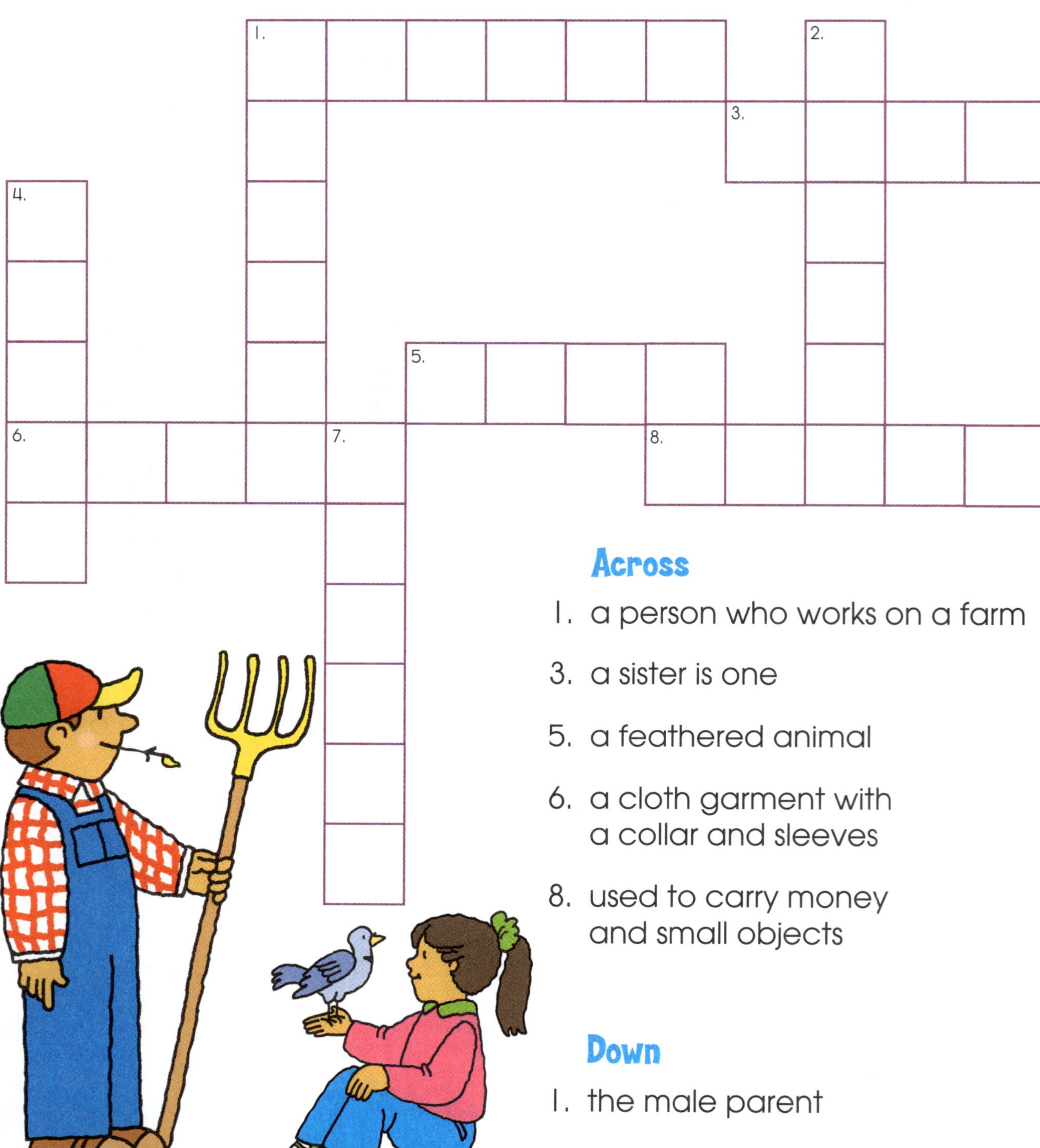

Across

1. a person who works on a farm
3. a sister is one
5. a feathered animal
6. a cloth garment with a collar and sleeves
8. used to carry money and small objects

Down

1. the male parent
2. one of three daily meals
4. a person who cares for the sick
7. a reptile with a shell

purse	farmer	nurse
father	shirt	dinner
bird	turtle	girl

COMBINATION SOUNDS: ew, oo

Read the clues.
Write the **ew** and **oo** words.

1. if + ood - i =
2. is + oon - i =
3. for + oom – fo =
4. it + ool – i =
5. in + ew – i =
6. now + ho – no =
7. mom + oon – mo =
8. ofl + ew – o =

Add the missing letters to make the **ew** and **oo** words from above.

9. n___ ___ 10. f___ ___d 11. wh___ 12. t___ ___l

13. fl___ ___ 14. m___ ___n 15. s___ ___n 16. r___ ___m

COMBINATION SOUNDS: ew, oo, ue

Write the **ew**, **oo**, and **ue** words to finish the sentences.

moon goose blew stew drew clues due few

1. The kids ____________ pictures on the sidewalk with chalk.

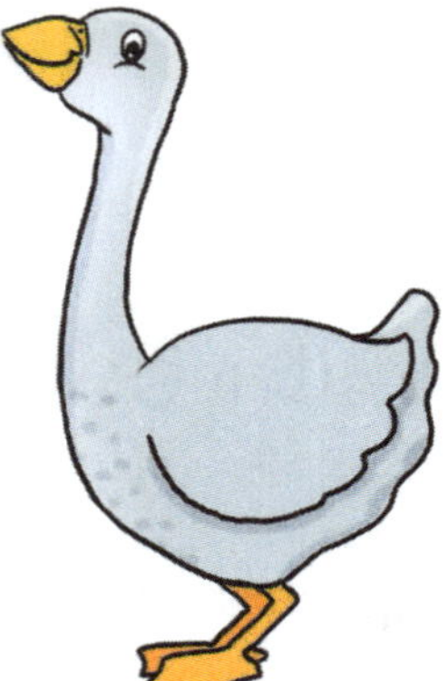

2. I saw a ____________ by the pond in the park.

3. Brett ____________ the biggest bubble.

4. The map gave us ____________ about where the treasure was hidden.

5. When is your library book ____________ ?

6. Your dad makes the best beef ____________ .

7. Robin loaned a ____________ of her books to me.

8. The astronaut hopes to visit the ____________ .

Write the **ew**, **oo**, and **ue** answers to the riddles.

stool	dew	broom	glue
chew	new	moose	blue
tooth	pool	school	true

1. It is the color of the sky. ____________________
2. You can find this on the grass in the morning. ____________________
3. Things stick together with it. ____________________
4. It is a big animal with antlers. ____________________
5. It is the opposite of old. ____________________
6. This is what you do with gum. ____________________
7. You can sit on it. ____________________
8. You can sweep the floor with it. ____________________
9. It is the opposite of false. ____________________
10. You should brush each ____________________ twice a day.
11. This is where you go to learn. ____________________
12. You go swimming in this. ____________________

boil joy point broil oil toy
soil moist join boy coin voice

1. Find the **oi** and **oy** words in the word search.

B	N	S	O	I	L	L	C	O	R	T
R	T	U	E	S	J	O	Y	L	F	O
O	L	N	B	P	E	I	N	B	O	Y
I	L	A	B	O	I	L	K	N	T	S
L	S	V	R	I	S	T	J	W	L	F
L	E	O	C	N	L	C	O	I	N	O
M	O	I	S	T	I	U	I	E	R	I
T	P	C	A	N	L	F	N	O	W	S
W	E	E	O	K	T	P	G	A	V	E

2. Write a sentence using an **oi** word.

3. Write a sentence using an **oy** word.

COMBINATION SOUNDS: oi, oy

Write the **oi** and **oy** words to finish the sentences.

boil	joy	oil	toys
moist	join	coins	voice

1. My mother's cake is always ____________.

2. Would you like to ____________ your opinion?

3. How long do you ____________ the corn?

4. The boy collects ____________.

5. Would you like to ____________ us for dinner?

6. My father changed the ____________ in his car.

7. My brother forgot to put away his ____________.

8. Anna is a ____________ to be around.

COMBINATION SOUNDS: ou, ow

Write the **ou** and **ow** words to finish the sentences.

about cow mouse now house flower owl out

1. The cat ran after the ______________.

2. I need to go home ______________.
3. What is the story ______________?
4. It is time to take the dog ______________ for a walk.

5. A ______________ is a farm animal.
6. Can you come to my ______________ after school?

7. The ______________ flies at night.
8. Penny put a ______________ in her hair.

Write the **ou** and **ow** answers to the riddles.

brown	crown	sour	hound
mouse	out	clown	howl

1. A lemon is this. ____________
2. Tree trunks are this color. ____________
3. A king wears one. ____________
4. This word means the opposite of in. ____________
5. A hunting dog is sometimes called this. ____________
6. This is a funny person in a circus. ____________
7. Wolves make this sound. ____________
8. It is a rodent with small ears and a long tail. ____________
9. Write a sentence using an **ou** word.

____

10. Write a sentence using an **ow** word.

____

REVIEW: BLENDS & COMBINATION SOUNDS

Write the **blend** and **combination sound** words to finish the sentences.

shell snail sticky creeps
plants ground shady groups

1. A ____________ has a soft body.

2. Its body is covered by a ____________ .

3. It ____________ along on a foot.

4. A ____________ slime helps them move.

5. Snails that live on land eat rotten ____________ .

6. They live in ____________ places.

7. Snails lay eggs in the ____________ .

8. Some ____________ of snails live in water.

REVIEW: BLENDS & COMBINATION SOUNDS

It is time for a school party.
Write the **blend** and **combination sound** words to finish the story.

black	flower	dressed	tricks	prize	blue
class	sprayed	clown	plan	stripes	shoes

Our ____________ is having a circus party.

Mr. Baker ____________ as a ____________.

He wore a ____________ shirt with ____________.

His ____________ were big and ____________.

The ____________ on his suspenders ____________ water.

We thought his ____________ were fun.

A ____________ was given for the funniest costume.

I think we should ____________ another party!

DIFFERENT SOUNDS: c, g

Copy the words. Say the words.

1. The letter **c** sounds like **k** before these vowels: **a**, **o**, and **u**.

cat ______________

cow ______________

cake ______________

cup ______________

2. The letter **c** sounds like **s** before these vowels: **i** and **e**.

city ______________

circus ______________

cent ______________

circle ______________

3. The letter **g** sounds like the **g** in goat before these vowels: **a**, **o**, and **u**.

gas ______________

gum ______________

good ______________

got ______________

4. The letter **g** usually sounds like **j** before these vowels: **i** and **e**.

general ______________

gem ______________

gentle ______________

giraffe ______________

SILENT LETTERS

Sometimes the letters **b**, **gh**, **h**, **k**, **l**, **t**, and **w** are silent.
Add the **silent letters** to finish the words.

1. **w**	2. **gh**	3. **b**	4. **t**
___rap	hi___ ___	dum___	ca___ch
___rong	si___ ___	thum___	ma___ch
___rite	ni___ ___t	crum___	swi___ch

5. **k**	6. **l**	7. **h**
___nob	wa___k	___onest
___nit	sta___k	___our
___nee	ta___k	g___ost

See if you can finish the words.

8. ri___ ___t	9. ___rite	10. ___onor
11. lam___	12. la___ch	13. bri___ ___t
14. ca___f	15. ___nock	16. ki___chen

SILENT LETTERS

As you've learned, sometimes the letters **b**, **gh**, **h**, **k**, **l**, **t**, and **w** are silent. Write the answers to the riddles, and underline the **silent letters**.

walk	calf	hour	dumb
knee	catch	wrong	night

1. opposite of right ____________________

2. opposite of day ____________________
3. not smart ____________________
4. opposite of throw ____________________
5. baby cow ____________________

6. opposite of run ____________________
7. 60 minutes of time ____________________
8. part of the leg ____________________

PREFIXES: un, mis

1. **Un** in front of a word means **not**.
   Finish the word puzzle using the prefix **un**.
   The first one is done for you.

not happy

not beaten

not clean

not clear

not fair

not seen

not tied

2. **Mis** in front of a word means **wrong**.
   Finish the word puzzle using the prefix **mis**.

wrong count

wrong place

wrong lead

wrong match

wrong take

wrong use

1. Finish the word puzzle using the prefix **un**.

not afraid

not able

not safe

not kind

not even

not known

2. Finish the word puzzle using the prefix **mis**.

wrong fit

wrong step

wrong deal

wrong fire

wrong fortune

wrong spelling

SUFFIXES: s, es

Plural means more than one. Here are some different ways to make words **plural**:
Write the words with the correct endings.

1. Sometimes you add **s**.

book	______________	clock	______________
hand	______________	flower	______________
doll	______________	mother	______________

2. When the word ends in **ch**, **sh**, **ss**, or **x**, you add **es**.

box	______________	pitch	______________
dress	______________	bench	______________
wish	______________	dish	______________

3. When the word ends in **y**, you change the **y** to **i** and add **es**.

baby	______________	cherry	______________
pony	______________	berry	______________
city	______________	penny	______________

4. When the word ends in **f**, you change the **f** to **v** and add **es**.
When the word ends in **fe**, you change the **f** to **v** and add **s**.

leaf	______________	knife	______________
wife	______________	shelf	______________

As you've learned, the ending **es** can be added to some words to name more than one.

If a word ends with a **consonant** and **y**, change the **y** to **i** and add **es**.

Write the words with the correct ending.

1. one baby

two 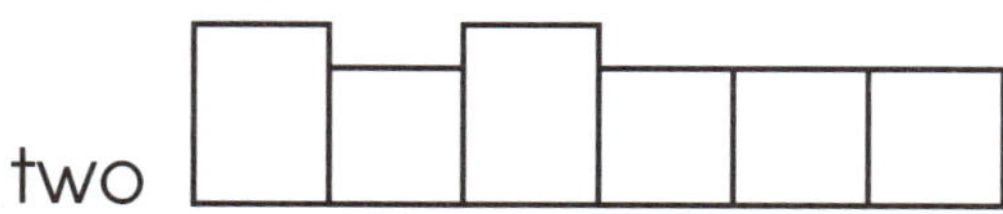

2. one penny

two 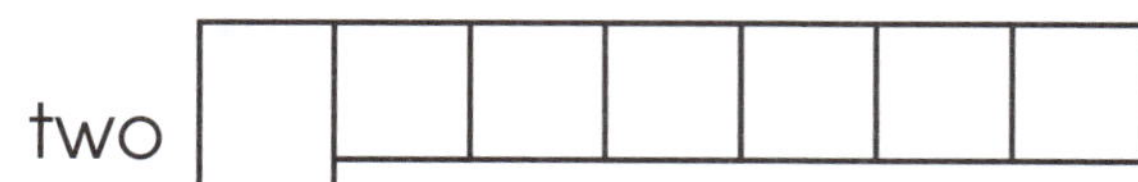

3. one berry

two 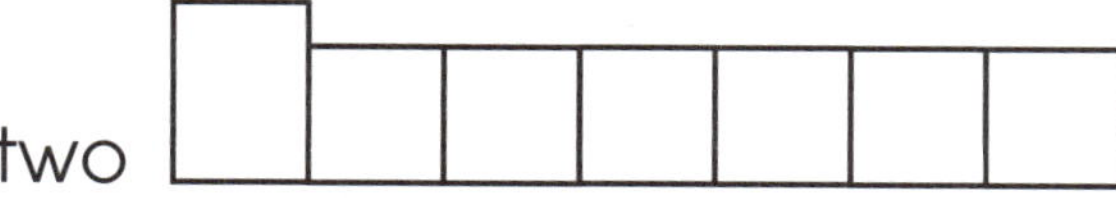

4. one candy

two 

5. one puppy

two 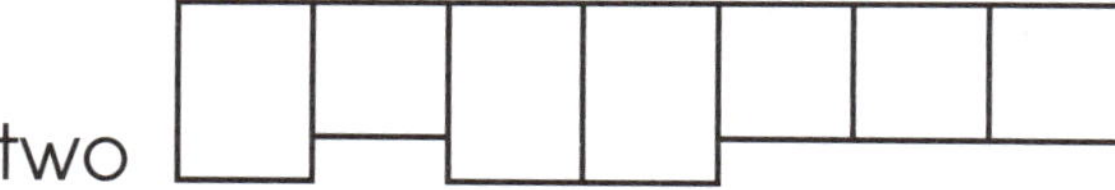

6. one butterfly

two 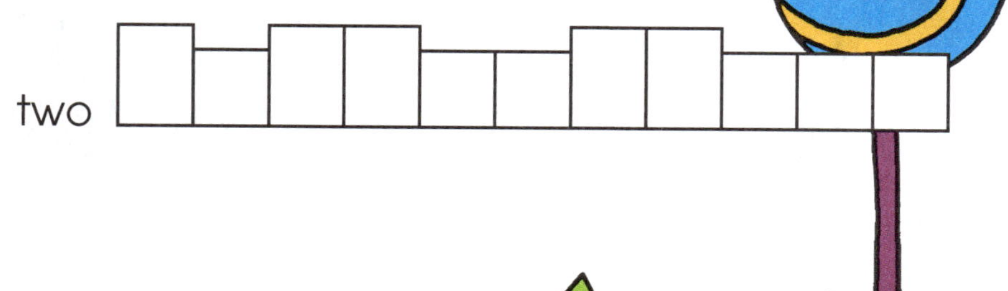

Write the words with the correct ending to finish the sentences.

city candy lady penny berry baby story cry

1. My sister ______________ when she can't come with me.
   cry

2. Use your ______________ to buy the gum.
   penny

3. How many ______________ have you visited?
   city

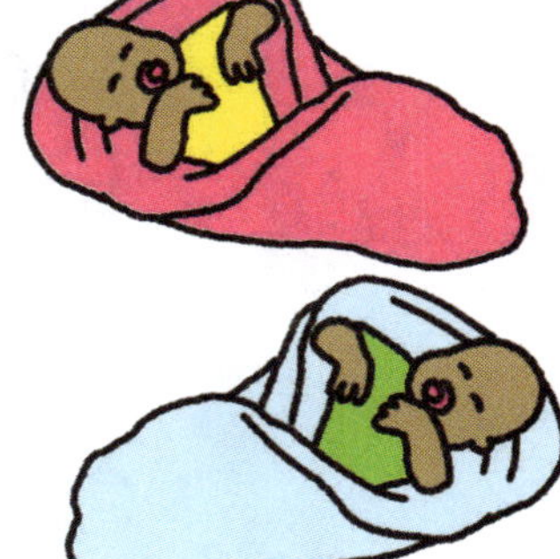

4. The ______________ are sleeping.
   baby

5. My mother and I picked lots of ______________.
   berry

6. The chocolate factory makes lots of sweet ______________.
   candy

7. The ______________ went shopping.
   lady

8. Will you read us some more ______________?
   story

As you've learned, you can add **s** or **es** to make a word name more than one. Add **s** to most words. Add **es** to words that end in **ch**, **sh**, or **x**.

foxes trees boxes inches bells dishes looks lunches

1. Look at the words above.
   Underline the words that have had **s** added.
   Circle the words that have had **es** added.

2. Find the following words in the word search.

toys tells wishes hogs bunches foxes looks pinches

```
F Q W B R T O Y S Y V D P
E R D U Z T H U P M B V I
H C V N M W I S H E S C N
O F T C Y H J K L M N B C
G B G H B I L Q A F R V H
S N H E Z P O Z X S W E E
I Y U S Y I O R E W S X S
K M J L P Y K F F V A Q Z
F O X E S H S B T E L L S
```

SUFFIXES: ed, ing

Some words end with one **vowel** and one **consonant**.
To get the **short vowel** sound, double the final **consonant** before adding **ed** or **ing**.

skip **grab**
hug **plan**

1. Write the words using the **ed** ending.

____

____

____

____

2. Write the words using the **ing** ending.

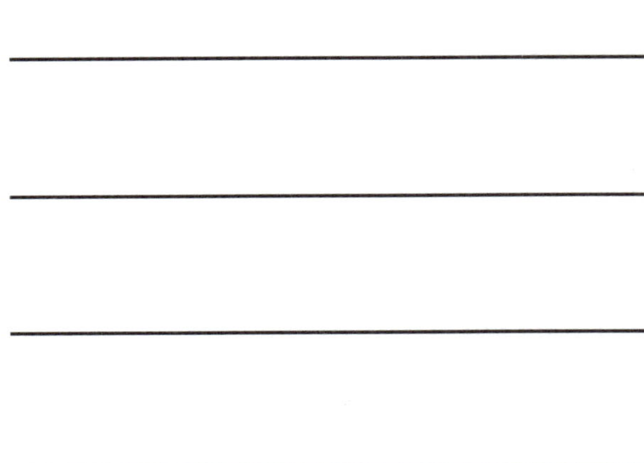

SUFFIXES: ed, ing

Write the words with the correct endings to finish the sentences.

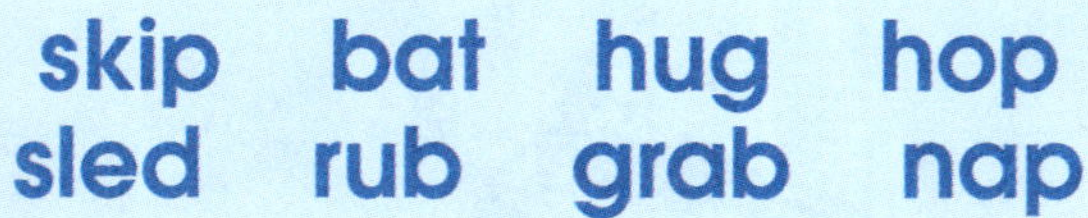

1. The rabbit ____________ into its hutch.
   hop

2. Jo ____________ in the winning run.
   bat

3. A good exercise is ____________ rope.
   skip

4. The baby is ____________ in her crib.
   nap

5. I ____________ the dish before it fell.
   grab

6. My bicycle tire is ____________ against the fender.
   rub

7. The players ____________ each other after the game.
   hug

8. The snow is perfect for ____________ .
   sled

If a word ends in **e**, drop the **e** and add **ing**.

like ⟶ liking

make	smile	use	race
hide	write	come	wash

Write the words with the correct ending to finish the sentences.

1. Sean is ____________ a poem.
   write

2. All of the runners were ____________ to the finish line.
   race

3. Raccoons like ____________ their faces.
   wash

4. Where was the cat ____________?
   hide

5. Dad is ____________ a dollhouse for me.
   make

6. The baby is ____________ at the dog.
   smile

7. We are ____________ a strong soap to clean it.
   use

8. Are you ____________ to the party?
   come

SUFFIXES: er, est, ful, ing, less, ness

Words can have different endings.
Write the words with the correct endings.

1. Add **ing**:

think ____________

sing ____________

work ____________

2. Double the last letter and add **ing**:

run ____________

swim ____________

jog ____________

3. Add **ness** or **less**:

sick ____________

care ____________

kind ____________

help ____________

4. Add **er** or **est**:

fast ____________

slow ____________

old ____________

hard ____________

5. Drop the **e** and add **ing**:

save ____________

make ____________

come ____________

6. Add **ful**:

care ____________

thank ____________

help ____________

CONTRACTIONS

When you use an apostrophe to put words together, you form a **contraction**.

Write the **contractions** to finish the sentences.

aren't	I'll	they'll
don't	isn't	they're
can't	We're	couldn't

1. The socks ______________ match.
   do not

2. I ______________ read her writing.
   could not

3. ______________ going on vacation tomorrow.
   We are

4. Hanna ______________ home.
   is not

5. ______________ bake cookies tonight.
   I will

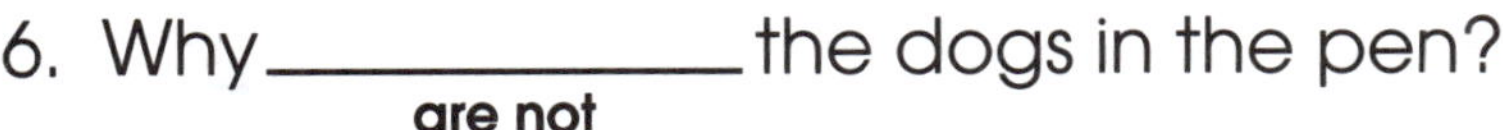

6. Why ______________ the dogs in the pen?
   are not

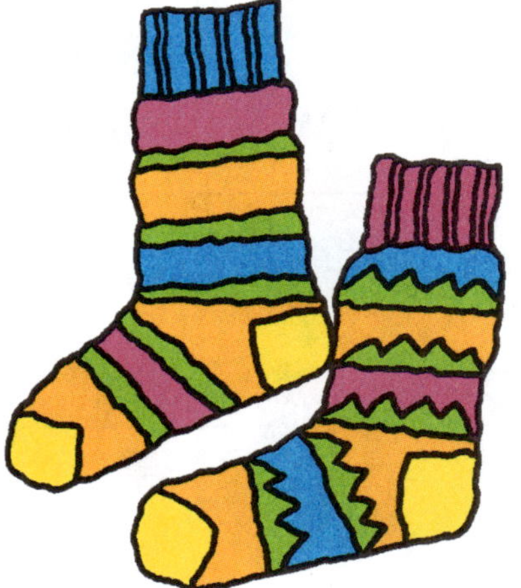

7. I was told ______________ on the way home.
   they are

8. Seth ______________ find his baseball.
   cannot

9. Our grandparents said ______________ see us on Saturday.
   they will

CONTRACTIONS

Write the **contractions** to finish the sentences.

I'll	aren't	couldn't
We're	isn't	they're
can't	don't	they'll

1. I ______________ find my book.
   could not

2. Dad ______________ find his watch.
   cannot

3. They said ______________ meet us there.
   they will

4. ______________ get the pizza for the party.
   I will

5. It ______________ time for the bus.
   is not

6. ______________ all tired from our soccer game.
   We are

7. They ______________ want to come with us.
   do not

8. Our dogs ______________ going with us.
   are not

9. Who said ______________ on the way back?
   they are

COMPOUND WORDS

Two words that are put together to make one word become a **compound word**.

Circle the words in the **compound words**. The first one is done for you.

1. **something**
2. **snowball**
3. **everywhere**
4. **anyone**
5. **inside**
6. **cannot**
7. **maybe**
8. **sunshine**
9. **herself**
10. **birthday**

Match words from the A list to words from the B list to make **compound words**. Write the **compound words** on the lines. The first one is done for you.

	A	+	B	
11.	moon		plane	______________
12.	rain		light	moonlight
13.	air		ground	______________
14.	foot		fly	______________
15.	butter		coat	______________
16.	play		ball	______________

COMPOUND WORDS

Let's practice making one word out of two! As you've learned, a **compound word** is two words put together to make one word.

 +  = birdhouse

Look at the pictures.
Write the **compound words**.

1.  +  = ______________

2. 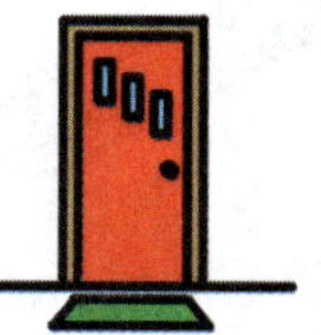 +  = ______________

3.   +  = ______________

4.  +  = ______________

5.  +  = ______________

6.  +  = ______________

7.  +  = ______________

8.  = ______________

NUMBER WORDS

1. Circle the words in the word search.

one two three four five six seven eight

W	J	T	Y	A	V	K	Q	V
Z	O	V	T	W	O	Z	T	S
Q	N	L	C	K	S	Q	H	E
T	E	T	S	I	X	X	R	V
H	Z	K	Z	A	D	L	E	E
F	L	F	O	U	R	C	E	N
I	K	X	J	R	N	K	J	P
V	P	U	E	I	G	H	T	V
E	X	W	Q	L	Q	H	X	I

2. Write the words as you find them in the puzzle.

1. Circle the words in the word search.

cat hat king ring boat coat dog frog

2. Write sentences using as many words from the puzzle as you can.

____

____

____

____

MORE RHYMING WORDS

1. Circle the words in the word search.

hen ten bin win van fan box fox

2. Write the words as you find them in the puzzle.

______________________ ______________________

______________________ ______________________

______________________ ______________________

______________________ ______________________

1. Circle the words in the word search.

tall short big little wet dry happy sad

S	A	D	K	S	H	O	R	T
Q	W	Z	N	M	G	C	L	V
H	A	P	P	Y	B	D	R	Y
Z	P	W	M	H	O	X	J	H
W	E	T	Z	F	T	A	L	L
T	H	C	X	V	N	R	Y	E
P	C	B	I	G	M	L	U	B
N	N	P	R	L	Q	X	C	L
A	L	I	T	T	L	E	K	O

2. Write sentences using as many words from the puzzle as you can.

____

____

____

____

MORE OPPOSITE WORDS

1. Circle the words in the word search.

stop go on off hot cold up down

A	F	B	Q	W	M	T	M	O
S	Q	Z	R	K	F	B	K	T
T	G	O	M	C	V	K	D	R
O	Q	U	H	R	O	N	Z	S
P	V	B	O	Z	F	M	Y	O
K	N	T	F	P	V	L	K	E
U	P	Z	F	X	C	O	L	D
Y	M	Q	Z	B	X	J	V	P
H	O	T	B	D	O	W	N	I

2. Write sentences using as many words from the puzzle as you can.

____

____

____

____

EVEN MORE OPPOSITE WORDS

1. Circle the words in the word search.

right left fast slow new old in out

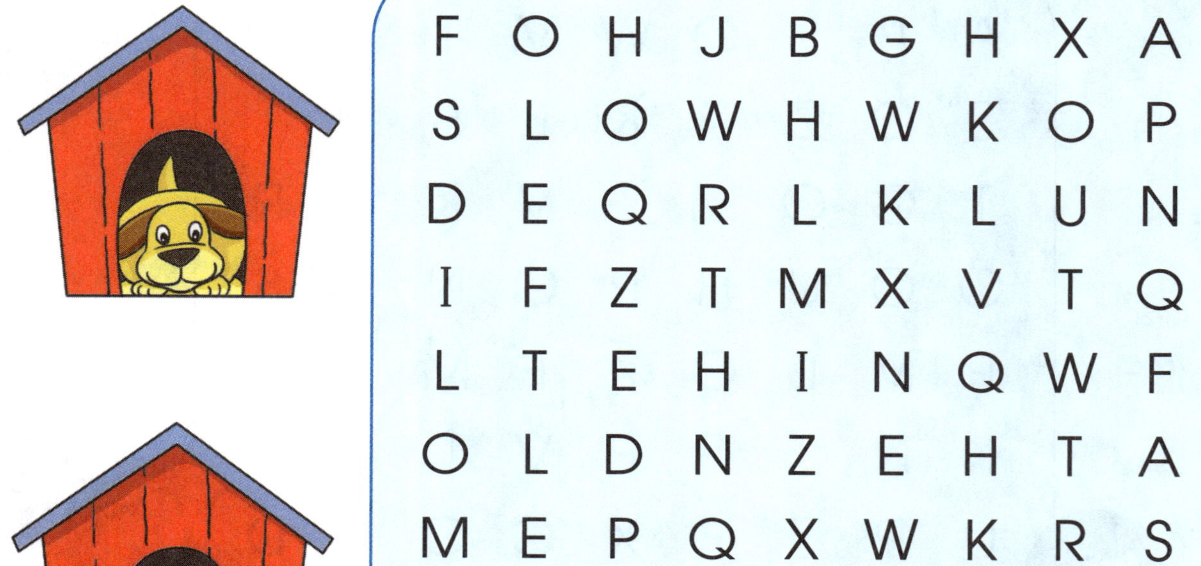

F	O	H	J	B	G	H	X	A
S	L	O	W	H	W	K	O	P
D	E	Q	R	L	K	L	U	N
I	F	Z	T	M	X	V	T	Q
L	T	E	H	I	N	Q	W	F
O	L	D	N	Z	E	H	T	A
M	E	P	Q	X	W	K	R	S
X	Q	Y	X	C	Z	Q	W	T
I	S	V	K	R	I	G	H	T

2. Write the words as you find them in the puzzle.

____________________ ____________________

____________________ ____________________

____________________ ____________________

____________________ ____________________

1. Circle the words in the word search.

carrot onion potato lettuce peas celery

A	C	P	C	E	L	E	R	Y
X	A	H	C	N	J	W	Q	P
L	R	F	B	O	N	I	O	N
E	R	K	H	K	Z	X	N	K
T	O	J	P	E	A	S	N	C
T	T	S	Z	W	R	P	M	M
U	F	U	M	J	T	V	K	R
C	P	O	T	A	T	O	Y	N
E	P	K	H	K	Q	Z	W	I

2. Write sentences using as many words from the puzzle as you can.

____

____

____

____

GARDEN CRITTER WORDS

1. Circle the words in the word search.

snail worm butterfly ant bee cricket snake

2. Write the words as you find them in the puzzle.

C WORDS

1. Circle the words in the word search.

cat cow cake car corn cup coat can

A C L K T C A K E
Q A Q M L T M C W
W T B C O W X C U
P Q L N B K P A B
O C O R N F W R F
V K K B S M Y R G
C Y C U P X K M Q
A Z N C W Z N T W
N P Z X L C O A T

2. Write sentences using as many words from the puzzle as you can.

___

___

___

___

1. Circle the words in the word search.

bird boat ball bus bed bee book

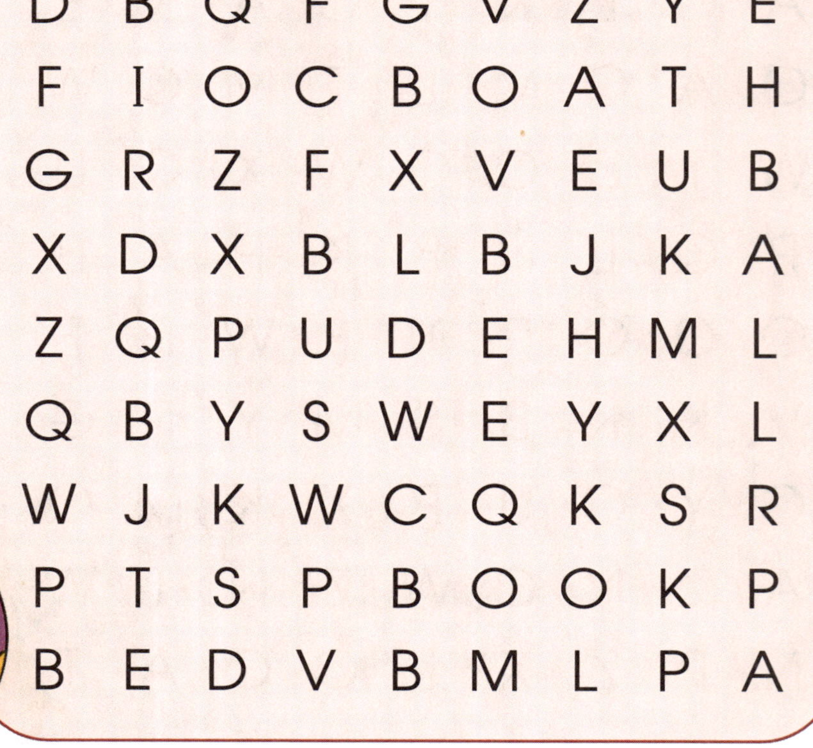

2. Write the words as you find them in the puzzle.

______________________ ______________________

______________________ ______________________

______________________ ______________________

______________________ ______________________

H WORDS

1. Circle the words in the word search.

hat happy ham hook heart hen house

A H A P P Y K X H
U R P K Q Y Q K A
H W H H O O K B T
A D G D X K D D H
M K H E A R T V R
Q Z D L K A K Q O
N C V R Q I G H V
Y H O U S E Q E F
I R J Q Z Q L N E

2. Write sentences using as many words from the puzzle as you can.

____

____

____

____

1. Circle the words in the word search.

dog dad drum duck doll dish day

2. Write the words as you find them in the puzzle.

1. Circle the words in the word search.

tennis skiing baseball soccer swimming

A	G	S	O	C	C	E	R	U
K	N	W	J	G	T	V	B	D
S	K	I	I	N	G	M	A	H
Q	X	M	D	B	J	Y	S	G
U	Z	M	Z	V	P	S	E	K
Z	C	I	Y	Q	P	L	B	L
T	E	N	N	I	S	K	A	Z
C	K	G	Z	F	M	H	L	X
I	H	D	N	M	Q	J	L	A

2. Write sentences using as many words from the puzzle as you can.

____

____

____

____

T WORDS

1. Circle the words in the word search.

top train tent tie tomato tiger tire toad

Q	T	R	A	I	N	H	V	C
M	L	P	J	C	Z	Q	Z	T
T	V	T	I	G	E	R	I	O
E	H	I	K	D	Z	M	T	A
N	T	R	V	X	K	Q	O	D
T	J	E	H	B	S	A	P	L
P	M	N	V	Z	T	Q	X	M
W	T	O	M	A	T	O	A	O
A	K	B	X	Z	O	T	I	E

2. Write the words as you find them in the puzzle.

P WORDS

1. Circle the words in the word search.

pig puppy pear pizza penny pie pen pet

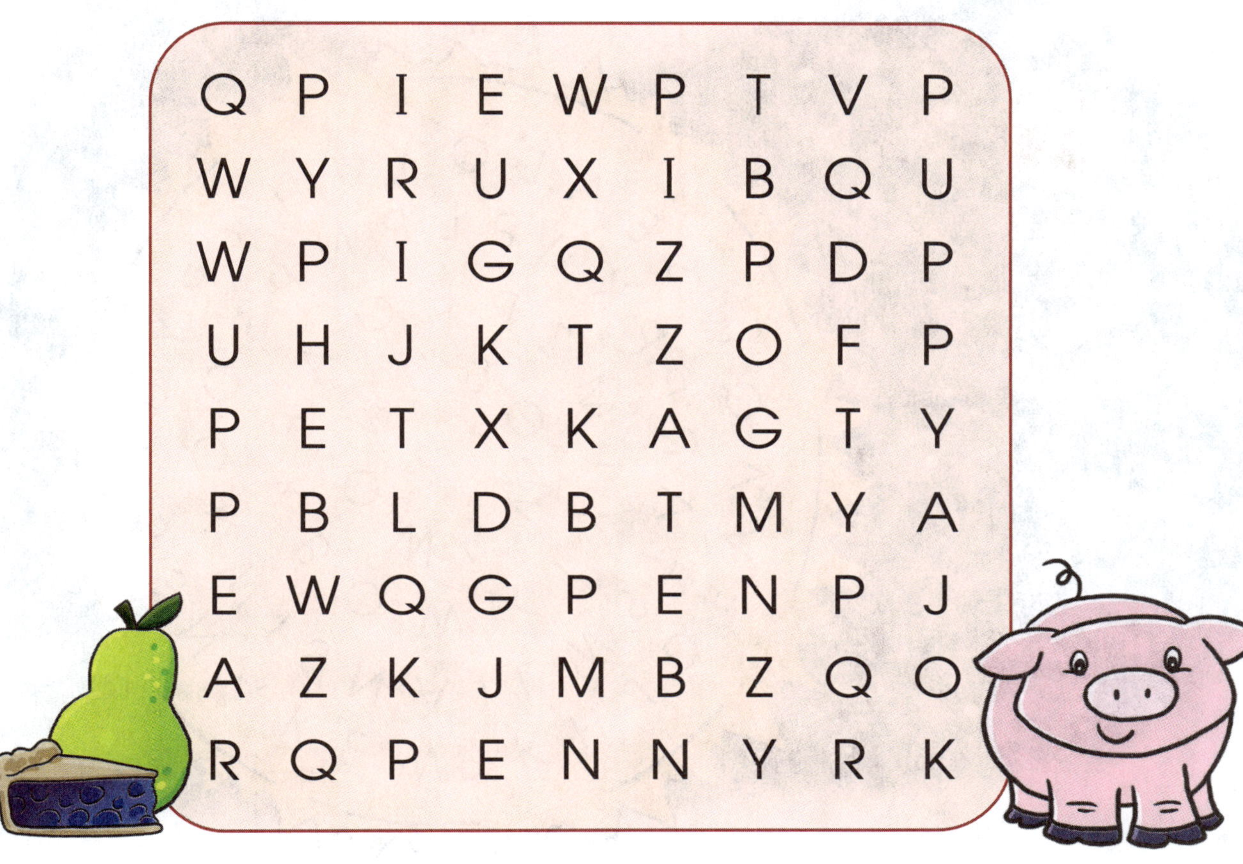

2. Write sentences using as many words from the puzzle as you can.

____

____

____

____

1. Circle the words in the word search.

sock **sun** **star** **seal** **snail** **soap** **snake**

2. Write the words as you find them in the puzzle.

______________________ ______________________

______________________ ______________________

______________________ ______________________

______________________ ______________________

1. Circle the words in the word search.

ladybug ant butterfly mosquito bee beetle

2. Write sentences using as many words from the puzzle as you can.

____

____

____

____

WINTER WEAR WORDS

1. Circle the words in the word search.

boots scarf hat coat mittens gloves

Q	W	S	C	A	R	F	L	K
B	V	B	H	J	L	M	W	G
O	B	H	A	T	B	Z	Q	L
O	P	L	W	X	Z	Q	F	O
T	N	M	C	V	K	U	X	V
S	N	X	C	O	A	T	Q	E
B	W	Q	P	I	B	C	Z	S
P	L	M	N	B	C	Z	R	T
A	M	I	T	T	E	N	S	E

2. Write the words as you find them in the puzzle.

______________________ ______________________

______________________ ______________________

______________________ ______________________

______________________ ______________________

CARNIVAL WORDS

1. Circle the words in the word search.

clown balloons games hats masks food prizes

2. Write sentences using as many words from the puzzle as you can.

1. Circle the words in the word search.

rain ring robot rose rug red robin rope

2. Write the words as you find them in the puzzle.

____________________ ____________________

____________________ ____________________

____________________ ____________________

____________________ ____________________

1. Circle the words in the word search.

panda seal bear tiger zebra lion elephant

2. Write sentences using as many words from the puzzle as you can.

____

____

____

____

FRUIT WORDS

1. Circle the words in the word search.

banana cherry orange pear lemon melon apple

2. Write the words as you find them in the puzzle.

1. Circle the words in the word search.

giraffe giant squid blue whale ostrich elephant

2. Write sentences using as many words from the puzzle as you can.

____

____

____

____

1. Circle the words in the word search.

dog saw bee pie jet car bed cat

2. Write the words as you find them in the puzzle.

________________ ________________

________________ ________________

________________ ________________

________________ ________________

FAST FOOD WORDS

1. Circle the words in the word search.

hamburger **hot dog** **pizza** **taco** **burrito** **fries**

H A M B U R G E R
J K T D B Z Y C F
H T A C O K F H R
V L J E M B K T I
Z B U R R I T O E
W X C Z F P B X S
Q P I Z Z A Q J T
L H B V Y S Z N U
E K H O T D O G O

2. Write sentences using as many words from the puzzle as you can.

____

____

____

____

1. Circle the words in the word search.

yellow blue orange red green brown purple black

2. Write the words as you find them in the puzzle.

____________________ ____________________

____________________ ____________________

____________________ ____________________

____________________ ____________________

FARM ANIMAL WORDS

1. Circle the words in the word search.

horse pig sheep goose goat cow hen

H	R	T	H	W	Q	B	N	E
V	M	X	G	M	P	I	G	R
R	Q	N	V	Z	G	F	O	T
H	G	K	C	H	M	G	O	U
E	O	Z	O	X	Z	T	S	L
N	A	B	W	S	H	E	E	P
V	T	E	G	Q	Y	C	G	M
P	H	O	R	S	E	Z	K	D
T	Z	C	Q	J	H	X	J	A

2. Write sentences using as many words from the puzzle as you can.

____

____

____

____

TRANSPORTATION WORDS

1. Circle the words in the word search.

car truck bike train bus van plane

2. Write the words as you find them in the puzzle.

DAYS OF THE WEEK WORDS

1. Circle the words in the word search.

Monday **Tuesday** **Wednesday**
Thursday **Friday** **Saturday** **Sunday**

S	Q	M	O	N	D	A	Y	E
A	T	H	U	R	S	D	A	Y
T	C	P	G	K	P	S	W	Q
U	R	Q	X	W	J	U	H	X
R	J	S	K	D	K	N	I	U
D	H	T	U	E	S	D	A	Y
A	D	C	H	V	L	A	M	X
Y	F	R	I	D	A	Y	N	F
W	E	D	N	E	S	D	A	Y

2. Write sentences using as many words from the puzzle as you can.

____

____

____

____

GROWING FLOWER WORDS

1. Circle the words in the word search.

flowers **seeds** **water** **sun** **roots** **soil**

Q	R	O	O	T	S	H	L	A
W	N	L	W	R	S	C	M	F
O	F	L	O	W	E	R	S	X
H	N	Q	Z	Q	E	O	P	Z
N	S	P	C	V	D	J	X	S
C	X	D	W	T	S	B	Z	O
K	C	M	N	B	M	S	J	I
L	G	V	G	X	B	U	Q	L
D	W	A	T	E	R	N	V	U

2. Write the words as you find them in the puzzle.

_______________ _______________

_______________ _______________

_______________ _______________

_______________ _______________

1. Circle the words in the word search.

triangle square diamond star rectangle oval circle

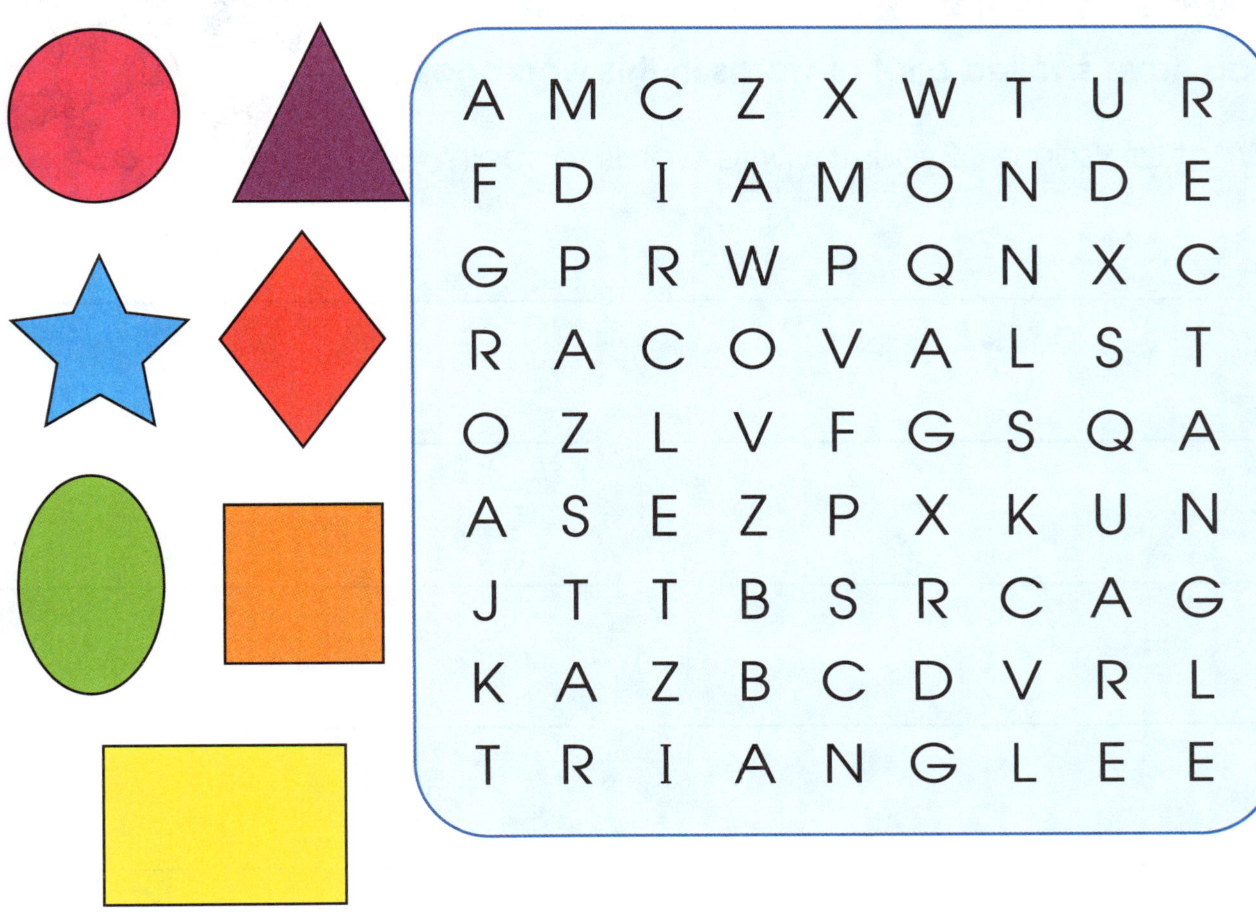

2. Write sentences using as many words from the puzzle as you can.

____

____

____

____

GREAT JOB!

You have spelled a lot of words in this workbook.

What are some of your favorite words to spell?